G000166805

AMSTERDAM
RESTAURANT GUIDE
2020

RESTAURANTS, BARS AND CAFES

Your Guide to Authentic Regional Eats

GUIDE BOOK FOR TOURIST

AMSTERDAM RESTAURANT GUIDE 2020
Restaurants, Bars & Cafés

© Herbert G. Newitz, 2020
© E.G.P. Editorial, 2020

Printed in USA.

ISBN-13: 9781080984510

AMSTERDAM RESTAURANT GUIDE 2020

Restaurants, Bars and Cafés in Amsterdam

This directory is dedicated to Amsterdam Business Owners and Managers who provide the experience that the locals and tourists enjoy. Thanks you very much for all that you do and thank for being the "People Choice".

Thanks to everyone that posts their reviews online and the amazing reviews sites that make our life easier.

The places listed in this book are the most positively reviewed and recommended by locals and travelers from around the world.

Thank you for your time and enjoy the directory that is designed with locals and tourist in mind!

TOP 500
RESTAURANTS
Ranked from #1 to #500

#1
Gartine
Category: Breakfast & Brunch
Average price: €8-20
Area: Centrum
Address: Taksteeg 7 1012 PB
Amsterdam The Netherlands
Phone: +31 20 3204132

#2
Vlaams Friteshuis Vleminckx
Category: Do-It-Yourself Food, Street
Vendors, Food Stands
Average price: Under €7
Area: Centrum
Address: Voetboogstraat 33 1012 XK
Amsterdam The Netherlands
Phone: +31 654 787000

#3
Restaurant Blauw
Category: Indonesian
Average price: €21-40
Area: Zuid
Address: Amstelveenseweg 158-160
1075 XN Amsterdam The Netherlands
Phone: +31 20 6755000

#4
De Kas
Category: Do-It-Yourself Food
Average price: Above €41
Area: Oost, Watergraafsmeer
Address: Kamerlingh Onneslaan 3
1097 DE Amsterdam The Netherlands
Phone: +31 20 4624562

#5
Winkel
Category: Soup, Seafood, Vegetarian
Average price: €8-20
Area: Centrum, Jordaan
Address: Noordermarkt 43 1015 NA
Amsterdam The Netherlands
Phone: +31 20 6230223

#6
Tales & Spirits
Category: Cocktail Bar, European
Average price: €21-40
Area: Centrum
Address: Lijnbaanssteeg 5-7 1012 TE
Amsterdam The Netherlands
Phone: +31 655 356467

#7
Scandinavian Embassy
Category: Coffee & Tea,
Scandinavian, Fashion
Average price: €8-20
Area: Zuid, De Pijp
Address: Sarphatipark 34 1072 PB
Amsterdam The Netherlands
Phone: +31 619 518199

#8
Café De Klos
Category: GastroPub, Steakhouses
Average price: €8-20
Area: Centrum
Address: Kerkstraat 41-II 1017 GB
Amsterdam The Netherlands
Phone: +31 20 6253730

#9
Cafe Brecht
Category: Bar, Cafe
Average price: €8-20
Area: Centrum
Address: Weteringschans 157 1017 SE
Amsterdam The Netherlands
Phone: +31 20 6272211

#10
Omelegg
Category: Breakfast & Brunch
Average price: €8-20
Area: Zuid, De Pijp
Address: Ferdinand Bolstraat 143
1072 LH Amsterdam The Netherlands
Phone: +31 20 3701134

#11
Mystique
Category: Bar, Diners
Average price: €21-40
Area: Centrum
Address: Utrechtsestraat 30a 1017 VN
Amsterdam The Netherlands
Phone: +31 20 3302994

#12
Moeders
Category: Salad, Soup
Average price: €8-20
Area: Centrum, Jordaan, West
Address: Rozengracht 251 1016 SX
Amsterdam The Netherlands
Phone: +31 20 6267957

#13
Brouwerij 't IJ
Category: Breweries, Cafe
Average price: Under €7
Area: Centrum
Address: Funenkade 7 1018 AL
Amsterdam The Netherlands
Phone: +31 20 6228325

#14
Café Bern
Category: Fondue, GastroPub
Average price: €8-20
Area: Centrum
Address: Nieuwmarkt 9 1011 JP
Amsterdam The Netherlands
Phone: +31 20 6220034

#15
Castell
Category: Steakhouses
Average price: €21-40
Area: Centrum
Address: Lijnbaansgracht 253 1017 RK
Amsterdam The Netherlands
Phone: +31 20 6228606

#16
Vis Aan De Schelde
Category: Seafood
Average price: €21-40
Area: Zuid, Rivierenbuurt
Address: Scheldeplein 4 1078 GR
Amsterdam The Netherlands
Phone: +31 20 6751583

#17
Pancakes! Amsterdam
Category: Creperies
Average price: €8-20
Area: Centrum, Negen Straatjes
Address: Berenstraat 38 1016 GH
Amsterdam The Netherlands
Phone: +31 20 5289797

#18
Pannenkoekenhuis Upstairs
Category: Creperies
Average price: €8-20
Area: Centrum, De Wallen
Address: Grimburgwal 2 1012 GA
Amsterdam The Netherlands
Phone: +31 20 6265603

#19
Burger-Bar
Category: Fast Food
Average price: €8-20
Area: Centrum
Address: Kolksteeg 2 1012 PT
Amsterdam The Netherlands
Phone: +31 20 6249049

#20
Balthazar's Keuken
Category: Mediterranean
Average price: €21-40
Area: Centrum, Jordaan
Address: Elandsgracht 108 1016 VA
Amsterdam The Netherlands
Phone: +31 20 4202114

#21
Bakers & Roasters
Category: Breakfast & Brunch, Cafe
Average price: €8-20
Area: Zuid, De Pijp
Address: Eerste Jacob van Campenstraat 54
1072 BH Amsterdam The Netherlands
Phone: +31 614 699645

#22
Café Loetje
Category: Steakhouses
Average price: €8-20
Area: Zuid, Museumkwartier
Address: Johannes Vermeerstraat 52-III 1071
DT Amsterdam The Netherlands
Phone: +31 20 6628173

#23
The Pancake Bakery
Category: Creperies
Average price: €8-20
Area: Centrum
Address: Prinsengracht 191 1015 DS
Amsterdam The Netherlands
Phone: +31 20 6251333

#24
**Belgisch Bierproeflokaal
De Zotte**
Category: Pub, Belgian
Average price: €8-20
Area: Centrum, Jordaan
Address: Raamstraat 29 1016 XL
Amsterdam The Netherlands
Phone: +31 20 6268694

#25
Yamazato
Category: Sushi Bar, Japanese
Average price: Above €41
Area: Zuid, De Pijp
Address: Yamazato Restaurant 1072 LH
Amsterdam The Netherlands
Phone: +31 20 6787450

#26
Bird
Category: Thai
Average price: €8-20
Area: Centrum, De Wallen
Address: Zeedijk 72 1012 BA
Amsterdam The Netherlands
Phone: +31 20 6201442

#27
Restaurant Koh-I-Noor
Category: Indian
Average price: €8-20
Area: Centrum
Address: Westermarkt 29 1016 DJ
Amsterdam The Netherlands
Phone: +31 20 6233133

#28
Warung Spang Makandra
Category: Diners, Indonesian,
Ethnic Food
Average price: €8-20
Area: Zuid, De Pijp
Address: Gerard Doustraat 39 1072 VK
Amsterdam The Netherlands
Phone: +31 20 6705081

#29
Seasons Restaurant
Category: Salad, Soup, European
Average price: €8-20
Area: Centrum
Address: Herenstraat 16 1015 CA
Amsterdam The Netherlands
Phone: +31 20 3303800

#30
Sugar & Spice Bakery
Category: Bakeries, Coffee & Tea,
Breakfast & Brunch
Average price: €8-20
Area: Centrum, De Wallen
Address: Zeedijk 75 1012 AS
Amsterdam The Netherlands
Phone: +31 686 045183

#31
La Boutique Del Caffe Torrefazione
Category: Coffee & Tea, Cafe
Average price: Under €7
Area: Zuid, De Pijp
Address: Eerste Jacob Van Campenstraat 38
Amsterdam, Noord-Holland
The Netherlands
Phone: +31 20 3640500

#33
Manneken Pis
Category: Fast Food
Average price: Under €7
Area: Centrum
Address: Damrak 41 1012 LK
Amsterdam The Netherlands
Phone: +31 20 6384568

#32
Kantjil & de Tijger
Category: Indonesian
Average price: €8-20
Area: Centrum
Address: Spuistraat 291-293 1012 VS
Amsterdam The Netherlands
Phone: +31 20 6200994

#34
The Pantry
Category: Creperies
Average price: €8-20
Area: Centrum
Address: Leidsekruisstraat 21-III 1017 RE
Amsterdam The Netherlands
Phone: +31 20 6200922

#35
De Pizzabakkers
Category: Pizza
Average price: €8-20
Area: Centrum, Haarlemmerbuurt
Address: Haarlemmerdijk 128-BG 1013 JJ
Amsterdam The Netherlands
Phone: +31 20 4274144

#36
Valerius
Category: Breakfast & Brunch, Sandwiches
Average price: €8-20
Area: Zuid, Museumkwartier
Address: Banstraat 14 1071 DP
Amsterdam The Netherlands
Phone: +31 20 4713976

#37
Coffee Bru
Category: Restaurant, Coffee & Tea
Average price: Under €7
Area: Oost, Oosterparkbuurt
Address: Beukenplein 14 1091 KG
Amsterdam The Netherlands
Phone: +31 20 7519956

#38
Latei
Category: Restaurant, Coffee & Tea
Average price: €8-20
Area: Centrum, De Wallen
Address: Zeedijk 143 1012 AW
Amsterdam The Netherlands
Phone: +31 20 6257485

#39
Thaise Snackbar Bird
Category: Thai
Average price: €8-20
Area: Centrum, De Wallen
Address: Zeedijk 77-I 1012 AS
Amsterdam The Netherlands
Phone: +31 20 4206289

#40
The Butcher
Category: Burgers
Average price: €8-20
Area: Zuid, De Pijp
Address: Albert Cuypstraat 129 1072 CS
Amsterdam The Netherlands
Phone: +31 20 4707875

#41
Foodism
Category: GastroPub, Food
Average price: €8-20
Area: West, Frederik Hendrikbuurt
Address: Nassaukade 122 1052 EC
Amsterdam The Netherlands
Phone: +31 20 4868137

#42
De Reiger
Category: Pub, Cafe
Average price: €8-20
Area: Centrum, Jordaan
Address: Nieuwe Leliestraat 34 1015 ST
Amsterdam The Netherlands
Phone: +31 20 6247426

#43
Hotel de Goudfazant
Category: Venues & Events
Average price: €21-40
Area: Noord
Address: Aambeeldstraat 10-H 1021 KB
Amsterdam The Netherlands
Phone: +31 20 6365170

#44
Restaurant PS
Category: Mediterranean
Average price: €21-40
Area: Centrum, Haarlemmerbuurt
Address: Planciusstraat 49 1013 ME
Amsterdam The Netherlands
Phone: +31 20 4215218

#45
Tempo Doeloe
Category: Indonesian
Average price: €21-40
Area: Centrum
Address: Utrechtsestraat 75 1017 VJ
Amsterdam The Netherlands
Phone: +31 20 6256718

#46
New King Mandarin Cuisine
Category: Chinese
Average price: €8-20
Area: Centrum
Address: Zeedijk 115-117 1012 AV
Amsterdam The Netherlands
Phone: +31 20 6252180

#47
La Oliva
Category: Tapas, Bagels
Average price: €21-40
Area: Centrum, Jordaan
Address: Egelantiersstraat 122-124
1015 PR Amsterdam The Netherlands
Phone: +31 20 3204316

#48
Wilde Zwijnen
Category: Diners
Average price: €21-40
Area: Oost, Indische Buurt
Address: Javaplein 23 hs 1095 CJ
Amsterdam The Netherlands
Phone: +31 20 4633043

#49
Wok to Walk
Category: Chinese
Average price: Under €7
Area: Centrum
Address: Kolksteeg 8 1012 PT
Amsterdam The Netherlands
Phone: +31 20 4276960

#50
Restaurant Incanto
Category: Italian
Average price: Above €41
Area: Centrum
Address: Amstel 2 1017 AA
Amsterdam The Netherlands
Phone: +31 20 4233681

#51
Tomaz
Category: Desserts, Diners
Average price: €8-20
Area: Centrum
Address: Begijnensteeg 6-8 1012 PN
Amsterdam The Netherlands
Phone: +31 20 3206489

#52
Van Kerkwijk
Category: Pub, GastroPub
Average price: €21-40
Area: Centrum, De Wallen
Address: Nes 41 1012 KC
Amsterdam The Netherlands
Phone: +31 20 6203316

#53
Restaurant Zaza's
Category: French
Average price: €21-40
Area: Zuid, De Pijp
Address: Daniel Stalpertstraat 103
1072 XD Amsterdam The Netherlands
Phone: +31 20 6736333

#54
Toos & Roos
Category: Cafe,
Breakfast & Brunch, European
Average price: €8-20
Area: Centrum
Address: Herengracht 309 1016 AV
Amsterdam The Netherlands
Phone: +31 641 366733

#55
Venkel
Category: Do-It-Yourself Food,
Organic Stores
Average price: €8-20
Area: Zuid, De Pijp
Address: Albert Cuypstraat 22 1072 CT
Amsterdam The Netherlands
Phone: +31 20 7723198

#56
Terra Zen Centre
Category: Japanese,
Caribbean, Vegan
Average price: €8-20
Area: Centrum
Address: 19 hs Sint Jacobstraat 1012 NC
Amsterdam The Netherlands
Phone: +31 684 851848

#57
Singel 404
Category: Breakfast & Brunch
Average price: €8-20
Area: Centrum
Address: Singel 404 1016 AK
Amsterdam The Netherlands
Phone: +31 20 4280154

#58
&Samhoud Places
Category: Lounge, European
Average price: €8-20
Area: Centrum
Address: Oosterdokskade 5 1011 AD
Amsterdam The Netherlands
Phone: +31 20 2602094

#59
't Zwaantje
Category: Cafe
Average price: €8-20
Area: Centrum, Negen Straatjes
Address: Berenstraat 12 1016 GH
Amsterdam The Netherlands
Phone: +31 20 6232373

#60
Amstel Hotel
Category: Hotel, Restaurant
Average price: Above €41
Area: Plantagebuurt, Centrum
Address: Professor Tulpplein 1 1018 GX
Amsterdam The Netherlands
Phone: +31 20 6226060

#61
Pasta e Basta
Category: Italian
Average price: €21-40
Area: Centrum
Address: Nieuwe Spiegelstraat 8-BG
1017 DE Amsterdam The Netherlands
Phone: +31 20 4222222

#62
Sampurna
Category: Indonesian
Average price: €8-20
Area: Centrum
Address: Singel 498-HS 1017 AX
Amsterdam The Netherlands
Phone: +31 20 6253264

#63
Bar Boca's
Category: European, Tapas
Average price: Under €7
Area: Centrum, Jordaan
Address: Westerstraat 30 1015 MK
Amsterdam The Netherlands
Phone: +31 20 8203727

#64
Bar Spek
Category: GastroPub
Average price: €8-20
Area: West, De Baarsjes
Address: Admiraal de Ruijterweg 1
1057 JT Amsterdam The Netherlands
Phone: +31 20 6188102

#65
The Taco Shop
Category: Tex-Mex, Vegetarian
Average price: €8-20
Area: Zuid, De Pijp
Address: Tolstraat 200 1074 HZ
Amsterdam The Netherlands
Phone: +31 20 4703657

#66
De Biertuin
Category: Cafe, Breweries
Average price: €8-20
Area: Oost, Dapperbuurt
Address: Linnaeusstraat 29 1093 EE
Amsterdam The Netherlands
Phone: +31 20 6650956

#67
Burger-Bar
Category: Fast Food, Burgers
Average price: €8-20
Area: Centrum
Address: Reguliersbreestraat 9
1017 CL Amsterdam The Netherlands
Phone: +31 20 3305968

#68
Tomatillo Tex-Mex TO GO
Category: Mexican
Average price: €8-20
Area: West, Oud West
Address: Overtoom 261 1054 HW
Amsterdam The Netherlands
Phone: +31 20 6833086

#69
Little Collins
Category: Breakfast & Brunch,
Diners, Bar
Average price: €8-20
Area: Zuid, De Pijp
Address: 1e Sweelinckstraat 19 F 1073 CL
Amsterdam The Netherlands
Phone: +31 20 6732293

#70
Wok to Walk
Category: Chinese
Average price: €8-20
Area: Centrum, De Wallen
Address: Warmoesstraat 85 1012 HZ
Amsterdam The Netherlands
Phone: +31 20 6250721

#71
Restaurant De Bolhoed
Category: Vegetarian
Average price: €8-20
Area: Centrum, Jordaan
Address: Prinsengracht 60-62 1015 DX
Amsterdam The Netherlands
Phone: +31 20 6261803

#72
The Seafood Bar
Category: Seafood
Average price: €21-40
Area: Zuid, Museumkwartier
Address: Van Baerlestraat 5 1071 AL
Amsterdam Oud Zuid The Netherlands
Phone: +31 20 6708355

#73
Hard Rock Cafe Amsterdam
Category: Pub, American, Food
Average price: €8-20
Area: Centrum
Address: Max Euweplein 57-61
1017 MA Amsterdam The Netherlands
Phone: +31 20 5237625

#74
Restaurant AS
Category: Diners, Wine Bar
Average price: Above €41
Area: Zuid, WTC
Address: Prinses Irenestraat 19 1077 WT
Amsterdam The Netherlands
Phone: +31 20 6440100

#75
Heavenly Made With Love/Tagore
Category: Indian, Cafe, Sandwiches
Average price: €8-20
Area: Centrum
Address: Utrechtsestraat 128 1017 VT
Amsterdam The Netherlands
Phone: +31 20 6241931

#76
The Dolphins Coffeeshop
Category: Cafe, Coffee & Tea
Average price: €8-20
Area: Centrum
Address: Kerkstraat 39 1017 GB
Amsterdam The Netherlands
Phone: +31 20 6259162

#77
Little Collins
Category: Breakfast & Brunch,
Diners, Bar
Average price: €8-20
Area: Zuid, De Pijp
Address: 1e Sweelinckstraat 19 F
1073 CL Amsterdam The Netherlands
Phone: +31 20 6732293

#78
Oriental City
Category: Dim Sum
Average price: €8-20
Area: Centrum, De Wallen
Address: Oudezijds Voorburgwal
177-179 1012 EV Amsterdam
The Netherlands
Phone: +31 20 6268352

#79
Thai Deum
Category: Thai
Average price: €8-20
Area: Zuid, De Pijp
Address: Ceintuurbaan 210-III BG
1072 GD Amsterdam The Netherlands
Phone: +31 20 3790705

#80
Red
Category: European
Average price: €21-40
Area: Centrum
Address: Keizersgracht 594 1017 EN
Amsterdam The Netherlands
Phone: +31 20 3201924

#81
Hannekes Boom
Category: GastroPub,
Jazz & Blues, Cafe, Pub
Average price: €8-20
Area: Centrum
Address: Dijksgracht 4 1019 BS
Amsterdam The Netherlands
Phone: +31 20 4199820

#82
d'Vijff Vlieghen
Category: European
Average price: Above €41
Area: Centrum
Address: Spuistraat 294-302
1012 VX Amsterdam The Netherlands
Phone: +31 20 5304060

#83
Bird Thais Restaurant
Category: Thai
Average price: €8-20
Area: Centrum, De Wallen
Address: Zeedijk 72- 74 1012 BA
Amsterdam The Netherlands
Phone: +31 20 6201442

#84
Burgermeester
Category: Burgers
Average price: €8-20
Area: Zuid, De Pijp
Address: Albert Cuypstraat 48
1072 CV Amsterdam The Netherlands
Phone: +31 20 6709339

#85
Harlem Soul Food
Category: Soul Food, Bar
Average price: €8-20
Area: Centrum, Haarlemmerbuurt
Address: Haarlemmerstraat 77 1013 EL
Amsterdam The Netherlands
Phone: +31 20 3301498

#86
Warung Mini Surinaams Eethuisje
Category: Diners, Ethnic Food,
Do-It-Yourself Food
Average price: €8-20
Area: Zuid, De Pijp
Address: Ceintuurbaan 205 1074 CV
Amsterdam The Netherlands
Phone: +31 20 6626804

#87
The Red Sun
Category: Japanese, Sushi Bar
Average price: Above €41
Area: Zuid, Stadionbuurt
Address: Olympiaplein 176 1076 AM
Amsterdam The Netherlands
Phone: +31 20 4707521

#88
Geisha
Category: Asian Fusion, Seafood
Average price: Above €41
Area: Centrum
Address: Prins Hendrikkade 106 A
1011 AJ Amsterdam The Netherlands
Phone: +31 20 6262410

#89
Envy
Category: European
Average price: €21-40
Area: Centrum, Negen Straatjes
Address: Prinsengracht 381 1016 HL
Amsterdam The Netherlands
Phone: +31 20 3446407

#90
Nam Kee
Category: Chinese
Average price: €8-20
Area: Centrum
Address: Geldersekade 117-HS
1011 EN Amsterdam The Netherlands
Phone: +31 20 6392848

#91
Brix Food 'n' Drinx
Category: Asian Fusion, Lounge
Average price: €8-20
Area: Centrum, Negen Straatjes
Address: Wolvenstraat 16 1016 EP
Amsterdam The Netherlands
Phone: +31 20 6390351

#92
l' Entrecôte et les Dames
Category: French
Average price: €21-40
Area: Zuid, Museumkwartier
Address: Van Baerlestraat 47 - 49
1071 AP Amsterdam The Netherlands
Phone: +31 20 6798888

#93
l' Entrecôte et les Dames
Category: French
Average price: €21-40
Area: Zuid, Museumkwartier
Address: Van Baerlestraat 47 - 49
1071 AP Amsterdam The Netherlands
Phone: +31 20 6798888

#94
Bazar
Category: Mediterranean, Arabian
Average price: €8-20
Area: Zuid, De Pijp
Address: Albert Cuypstraat 182 1073 BL
Amsterdam The Netherlands
Phone: +31 20 6750544

#95
Trouw Amsterdam
Category: Dance Club, Venues & Events,
Mediterranean
Average price: €8-20
Area: Oost, Oosterparkbuurt
Address: Wibautstraat 131 1091 GL
Amsterdam The Netherlands
Phone: +31 20 4637788

#96
Soup en Zo
Category: Do-It-Yourself Food
Average price: €8-20
Area: Centrum
Address: Nieuwe Spiegelstraat 54
1017 DG Amsterdam The Netherlands
Phone: +31 20 3307781

#97
Bridges
Category: Seafood, French
Average price: Above €41
Area: Centrum, De Wallen
Address: Oudezijds Voorburgwal 197
1012 EX Amsterdam The Netherlands
Phone: +31 20 5553560

#98
Cafe Kingfisher
Category: Pub, GastroPub
Average price: €8-20
Area: Zuid, De Pijp
Address: Ferdinand Bolstraat 24-II
1072 LK Amsterdam The Netherlands
Phone: +31 20 6712395

#99
Vinnies Deli
Category: Delis, Caterers
Average price: €8-20
Area: Centrum, Haarlemmerbuurt
Address: Haarlemmerstraat 46 1013 ES
Amsterdam The Netherlands
Phone: +31 20 7713086

#100
Burgermeester
Category: Burgers
Average price: €8-20
Area: Plantagebuurt, Centrum
Address: Plantage Kerklaan 37
1018 CV Amsterdam The Netherlands
Phone: +31 20 4280211

#101
Letting
Category: Sandwiches
Average price: €8-20
Area: Centrum
Address: Prinsenstraat 3 1015 DA
Amsterdam The Netherlands
Phone: +31 20 6279393

#102
Restaurant Blauw Aan De Wal
Category: French, European, Mediterranean
Average price: Above €41
Area: Centrum, De Wallen
Address: Oudezijds Achterburgwal 99
1012 DD Amsterdam The Netherlands
Phone: +31 20 3302257

#103
Elkaar
Category: French
Average price: €21-40
Area: Plantagebuurt, Centrum
Address: Alexanderplein 6 1018 CG
Amsterdam The Netherlands
Phone: +31 20 3307559

#104
Juice&Salad Café
Category: Salad, Vegetarian, Sandwiches
Average price: €8-20
Area: Centrum
Address: Vijzelstraat 135 1017 HJ
Amsterdam The Netherlands
Phone: +31 20 3303114

#105
Roopram Roti
Category: Caribbean
Average price: Under €7
Area: Oost, Dapperbuurt
Address: Eerste van Swindenstraat 4
1093 GC Amsterdam The Netherlands
Phone: +31 20 6932902

#106
Pacific Parc
Category: GastroPub
Average price: €8-20
Area: West
Address: Polonceau-kade 23 1014 DA
Amsterdam The Netherlands
Phone: +31 20 4887778

#107
ManaMana
Category: Middle Eastern
Average price: €21-40
Area: Zuid, De Pijp
Address: Hemonystraat 66hs 1074 BT
Amsterdam The Netherlands
Phone: +31 641 631098

#108
Sluizer
Category: European, Seafood
Average price: €21-40
Area: Centrum
Address: Utrechtsestraat 45 1017 VH
Amsterdam The Netherlands
Phone: +31 20 6226376

#109
De Belhamel
Category: French
Average price: €21-40
Area: Centrum, Haarlemmerbuurt
Address: Brouwersgracht 60-C 1013 GX
Amsterdam The Netherlands
Phone: +31 20 6221095

#110
BUFFET Van Odette
Category: Mediterranean, Bistros
Average price: €8-20
Area: Centrum
Address: Prinsengracht 598 1017 KS
Amsterdam The Netherlands
Phone: +31 20 4236034

#111
Café 't Sluisje
Category: GastroPub
Average price: Under €7
Area: Noord
Address: Nieuwendammerdijk 297-HS
1025 LM Amsterdam The Netherlands
Phone: +31 20 6361712

#112
Lombardo's
Category: Specialty Food, Beer,
Wine & Spirits, Burgers
Average price: €8-20
Area: Centrum
Address: Nieuwe Spiegelstraat 50
1017 DG Amsterdam The Netherlands
Phone: +31 20 4205010

#113
Japanese Pancake World
Category: Japanese
Average price: €8-20
Area: Centrum, Jordaan
Address: Tweede Egelantiersdwarsstraat
24a 1015 SC Amsterdam The Netherlands
Phone: +31 20 3204447

#114
Panini
Category: Italian
Average price: €8-20
Area: Centrum
Address: Vijzelgracht 3-5 1017 HM
Amsterdam The Netherlands
Phone: +31 20 6264939

#115
Maoz
Category: Middle Eastern, Vegetarian
Average price: Under €7
Area: Centrum
Address: Leidsestraat 85 1017 NX
Amsterdam The Netherlands
Phone: +31 20 6253913

#116
Hutspot
Category: Art Gallery, Cafe
Average price: €21-40
Area: Zuid, De Pijp
Address: Van Woustraat 4 1073 LL
Amsterdam The Netherlands
Phone: +31 613 651566

#117
Villa Zeezicht
Category: GastroPub, Food
Average price: €8-20
Area: Centrum
Address: Torensteeg 7 1012 TH
Amsterdam The Netherlands
Phone: +31 20 6267433

#118
Café Kiebêrt
Category: French,
Breakfast & Brunch, Cafe
Average price: €21-40
Area: Zuid, Stadionbuurt
Address: Marathonweg 2 1076 TE
Amsterdam The Netherlands
Phone: +31 20 8458283

#119
Gebroeders Niemeijer
Category: Bakeries, French,
Breakfast & Brunch
Average price: €8-20
Area: Centrum
Address: Nieuwendijk 35 1012 MA
Amsterdam The Netherlands
Phone: +31 20 7076752

#120
Los Pilones
Category: Mexican
Average price: €21-40
Area: Centrum
Address: Kerkstraat 63 1017 GC
Amsterdam The Netherlands
Phone: +31 20 3204651

#121
Frenzi
Category: Italian, European
Average price: €21-40
Area: Centrum
Address: Zwanenburgwal 232 1011 JH
Amsterdam The Netherlands
Phone: +31 20 4235112

#122
Greetje
Category: Local Flavor, Restaurant
Average price: €21-40
Area: Centrum
Address: Peperstraat 23 1011 TJ
Amsterdam The Netherlands
Phone: +31 20 7797450

#123
Restaurant De Struisvogel
Category: French
Average price: €8-20
Area: Centrum, Negen Straatjes
Address: Keizersgracht 312 1016 EX
Amsterdam The Netherlands
Phone: +31 20 4233817

#124
Zuivere Koffie
Category: Breakfast & Brunch
Average price: €8-20
Area: Centrum
Address: Utrechtsestraat 39 1017 VH
Amsterdam The Netherlands
Phone: +31 20 6249999

#125
Cafe Kostverloren
Category: Coffee & Tea,
Breakfast & Brunch, Diners
Average price: €8-20
Area: West, Oud West, Kinkerbuurt
Address: Tweede Kostverlorenkade 70
1053 SB Amsterdam The Netherlands
Phone: +31 20 8203161

#126
Mata Hari
Category: Bar, Mediterranean
Average price: €8-20
Area: Centrum, De Wallen
Address: Oudezijds Achterburgwal 22
1012 DM Amsterdam The Netherlands
Phone: +31 20 2050919

#127
Restaurant Fraîche
Category: European,
Breakfast & Brunch
Average price: €8-20
Area: Centrum, Jordaan
Address: Westerstraat 264 1015 MT
Amsterdam The Netherlands
Phone: +31 20 6279932

#128
Koffiehuis De Hoek
Category: Breakfast & Brunch, Cafe
Average price: Under €7
Area: Centrum, Negen Straatjes
Address: Prinsengracht 341 1016 HK
Amsterdam The Netherlands
Phone: +31 20 6253872

#129
Restaurant Mantoe
Category: Afghan
Average price: Above €41
Area: Centrum, Jordaan
Address: Tweede Leliedwarsstraat
13-BG 1015 TB Amsterdam
The Netherlands
Phone: +31 20 4216374

#130
Bloem 36
Category: GastroPub
Average price: €8-20
Area: Centrum
Address: Entrepotdok 36 1018 AD
Amsterdam The Netherlands
Phone: +31 20 3300929

#131
Fyra
Category: Salad, Soup, French
Average price: Above €41
Area: Centrum
Address: Noorderstraat 19-23
1017 TR Amsterdam The Netherlands
Phone: +31 20 4283632

#132
Sie-Joe
Category: Indonesian
Average price: €8-20
Area: Centrum
Address: Gravenstraat 24A 1012 NM
Amsterdam The Netherlands
Phone: +31 20 6241830

#133
De Haven Van Texel
Category: GastroPub
Average price: €8-20
Area: Centrum, De Wallen
Address: Sint Olofssteeg 11 1012 AK
Amsterdam The Netherlands
Phone: +31 20 4270768

#134
Small World Catering
Category: Breakfast & Brunch
Average price: €8-20
Area: Centrum, Haarlemmerbuurt
Address: Binnen Oranjestraat 14 1013 JA
Amsterdam The Netherlands
Phone: +31 20 4202774

#135
Van Dobben
Category: GastroPub
Average price: Under €7
Area: Centrum
Address: Korte Reguliersdwarsstraat 5
1017 BH Amsterdam The Netherlands
Phone: +31 20 6244200

#136
Maoz
Category: Middle Eastern
Average price: Under €7
Area: Centrum
Address: Damrak 40 1012 LK
Amsterdam The Netherlands
Phone: +31 20 4509987

#137
SLA
Category: Salad
Average price: €8-20
Area: Zuid, De Pijp
Address: Ceintuurbaan 149 1072 GB
Amsterdam The Netherlands
Phone: +31 20 7893080

#138
Brasserie Van Baerle
Category: Brasseries
Average price: €21-40
Area: Zuid, Museumkwartier
Address: Van Baerlestraat 158 1071 BG
Amsterdam The Netherlands
Phone: +31 20 6791532

#139
Café Reuring
Category: GastroPub,
French, European
Average price: €8-20
Area: Zuid, De Pijp
Address: Lutmastraat 99 1073 GR
Amsterdam The Netherlands
Phone: +31 20 7770996

#140
Wolvenstraat
Category: Asian Fusion
Average price: €8-20
Area: Centrum, Negen Straatjes
Address: Wolvenstraat 23 1016 EP
Amsterdam The Netherlands
Phone: +31 20 3200843

#141
Ciel Bleu
Category: French
Average price: Above €41
Area: Zuid, De Pijp
Address: Ferdinand Bolstraat 333 1072 LH
Amsterdam The Netherlands
Phone: +31 20 6787450

#142
Café Kadijk
Category: Diners, GastroPub, Bar
Average price: €8-20
Area: Centrum
Address: Kadijksplein 5 1018 AB
Amsterdam The Netherlands
Phone: +31 617 744411

#143
Haesje Claes
Category: Salad, Seafood
Average price: €8-20
Area: Centrum
Address: Spuistraat 269-BG 1012 VR
Amsterdam The Netherlands
Phone: +31 20 6251535

#144
Caffè Toscanini
Category: Italian
Average price: €21-40
Area: Centrum, Jordaan
Address: Lindengracht 75 1015 KD
Amsterdam The Netherlands
Phone: +31 20 6232813

#145
Restaurant Bussia
Category: Italian
Average price: €21-40
Area: Centrum, Negen Straatjes
Address: Reestraat 28-32 1016 DN
Amsterdam The Netherlands
Phone: +31 20 6278794

#146
Mamouche
Category: Moroccan
Average price: €21-40
Area: Zuid, De Pijp
Address: Quellijnstraat 104 1072 XZ
Amsterdam The Netherlands
Phone: +31 20 6700736

#147
'Skek
Category: GastroPub
Average price: €8-20
Area: Centrum, De Wallen
Address: Zeedijk 4 - 8 1012 AX
Amsterdam The Netherlands
Phone: +31 20 4270551

#148
Bistro Bij Ons
Category: GastroPub
Average price: €8-20
Area: Centrum
Address: Prinsengracht 287 1016 GW
Amsterdam The Netherlands
Phone: +31 20 6279016

#149
Restaurant - Café In de Waag
Category: Diners, Breakfast & Brunch
Average price: €8-20
Area: Centrum, De Wallen
Address: Nieuwmarkt 4 1012 CR
Amsterdam The Netherlands
Phone: +31 20 4227772

#150
La Place, V&D Kalverstraat
Category: Buffets
Average price: €8-20
Area: Centrum
Address: Kalverstraat 201-203
1012 XC Amsterdam The Netherlands
Phone: +31 20 6202364

#151
Sama Sebo
Category: Indonesian
Average price: €21-40
Area: Zuid, Museumkwartier
Address: P Cornelisz Hooftstr 27
1071 BL Amsterdam The Netherlands
Phone: +31 20 6628146

#152
Café-Restaurant Amsterdam
Category: Cafe
Average price: €8-20
Area: West, Bos en Lommer
Address: Watertorenplein 6 1051 PA
Amsterdam The Netherlands
Phone: +31 20 6822666

#153
Café Toussaint
Category: French, Cafe
Average price: €8-20
Area: West, Helmersbuurt
Address: Bosboom Toussaintstraat 26
1054 AS Amsterdam The Netherlands
Phone: +31 20 6850737

#154
Pata Negra
Category: Tapas, Spanish, Tapas Bar
Average price: €8-20
Area: Centrum
Address: Utrechtsestraat 124 1017 VT
Amsterdam The Netherlands
Phone: +31 20 4226250

#155
Bolenius
Category: European
Average price: Above €41
Area: Zuid, WTC, Buitenveldert
Address: George Gershwinlaan 30
1082 MT Amsterdam The Netherlands
Phone: +31 20 4044411

#156
Los Pilones
Category: Mexican
Average price: €21-40
Area: Centrum, Jordaan
Address: Eerste Anjeliersdwarsstraat 6
1015 NR Amsterdam The Netherlands
Phone: +31 20 6200323

#157
Brandstof
Category: Pub, Restaurant
Average price: €8-20
Area: Centrum, Jordaan
Address: Marnixstraat 341 1016 TD
Amsterdam The Netherlands
Phone: +31 20 4220813

#158
Sumo Amsterdam
Category: Sushi Bar, Japanese
Average price: €8-20
Area: Centrum
Address: Korte Leidsedwarsstraat
51-BG 1017 PW Amsterdam
The Netherlands
Phone: +31 20 4235131

#159
Café Schuim
Category: Pub, Sandwiches
Average price: €8-20
Area: Centrum
Address: Spuistraat 189 1012 VN
Amsterdam The Netherlands
Phone: +31 20 6389357

#160
Dynasty
Category: Chinese, Asian Fusion
Average price: Above €41
Area: Centrum
Address: Reguliersdwarsstraat 30
1017 BM Amsterdam The Netherlands
Phone: +31 20 6268400

#161
Petit Gateau
Category: Restaurant, Bakeries
Average price: €8-20
Area: Centrum, Haarlemmerbuurt
Address: Haarlemmerstraat 80 1013 EV
Amsterdam The Netherlands
Phone: +31 624 205631

#162
Thai & Co
Category: Thai
Average price: €8-20
Area: Centrum, Haarlemmerbuurt
Address: Haarlemmerstraat 54-BG
1013 ES Amsterdam The Netherlands
Phone: +31 20 6127324

#163
La Vallade
Category: French, Vegetarian
Average price: €21-40
Area: Oost, Oosterparkbuurt
Address: Ooster Ringdijk 23 1097 AB
Amsterdam The Netherlands
Phone: +31 20 6652025

#164
Vinkeles
Category: French
Average price: Above €41
Area: Centrum, Negen Straatjes
Address: Keizersgracht 384 1016 GB
Amsterdam The Netherlands
Phone: +31 20 5302010

#165
OCHA
Category: Thai
Average price: €8-20
Area: Centrum, De Wallen
Address: Binnen Bantammerstraat 1 1011
CH Amsterdam The Netherlands
Phone: +31 20 6259958

#166
Sushi Japans Eetcafé
Category: Japanese, Sushi Bar
Average price: €8-20
Area: Centrum
Address: Taksteeg 3-BG 1012 PB
Amsterdam The Netherlands
Phone: +31 20 4228978

#167
Lunchcafé Nielsen
Category: Breakfast & Brunch
Average price: €8-20
Area: Centrum, Negen Straatjes
Address: Berenstraat 19 1016 GG
Amsterdam The Netherlands
Phone: +31 20 3306006

#168
Golden Temple
Category: Vegetarian
Average price: €8-20
Area: Centrum
Address: Utrechtsestraat 126 1017 VT
Amsterdam The Netherlands
Phone: +31 20 6268560

#169
Burgermeester
Category: Burgers
Average price: €8-20
Area: Centrum, Jordaan
Address: Elandsgracht 130 1016 VB
Amsterdam The Netherlands
Phone: +31 20 6207437

#170
Xinh
Category: Vietnamese
Average price: €8-20
Area: Centrum, Jordaan
Address: Elandsgracht 2 1016 TV
Amsterdam The Netherlands
Phone: +31 20 6240308

#171
De Compagnon
Category: French, Diners
Average price: €21-40
Area: Centrum, De Wallen
Address: Guldehandsteeg 17
1012 RA Amsterdam The Netherlands
Phone: +31 20 6204225

#172
Bar Moustache
Category: Bar, Italian
Average price: €8-20
Area: Centrum
Address: Utrechtsestraat 141
1017 VM Amsterdam The Netherlands
Phone: +31 20 4281074

#173
Wok to Walk
Category: Chinese
Average price: Under €7
Area: Centrum
Address: Leidsestraat 96 1017 PE
Amsterdam The Netherlands
Phone: +31 20 6250721

#174
Café George
Category: French
Average price: €21-40
Area: Centrum, Jordaan
Address: Leidsegracht 84 1016 CR
Amsterdam The Netherlands
Phone: +31 20 6260802

#175
Rose's Cantina
Category: Mexican, Food
Average price: €8-20
Area: Centrum
Address: Reguliersdwarsstraat 38-40
1017 BM Amsterdam The Netherlands
Phone: +31 20 6259797

#176
Mi Sueno
Category: Argentine
Average price: €21-40
Area: Zuid, Rivierenbuurt
Address: Maasstraat 40 1078 HK
Amsterdam The Netherlands
Phone: +31 20 4711103

#177
Restaurant Utrechtsedwarstafel
Category: European, Salad
Average price: Above €41
Area: Centrum
Address: Utrechtsedwarsstraat 107-109
1017 WD Amsterdam The Netherlands
Phone: +31 20 6254189

#178
Meidi - Ya
Category: Japanese,
Grocery, Sushi Bar
Average price: €21-40
Area: Zuid, Apollobuurt
Address: Beethovenstraat 18-20 1077 HL
Amsterdam The Netherlands
Phone: +31 20 4004370

#179
Grekas Griekse Traiterie
Category: Greek
Average price: €8-20
Area: Centrum
Address: Singel 311 1012 WJ
Amsterdam The Netherlands
Phone: +31 20 6203590

#180
Aan de Amstel
Category: French
Average price: €8-20
Area: Oost, Oosterparkbuurt
Address: Weesperzijde 42-A 1091 EE
Amsterdam The Netherlands
Phone: +31 20 6080077

#181
Stadscafe Van Mechelen
Category: Dive Bar, Restaurant
Average price: €8-20
Area: Zuid, Hoofddorppleinbuurt
Address: Sloterkade 96-97 1058 HK
Amsterdam The Netherlands
Phone: +31 20 2212348

#182
Brasserie Baton
Category: Sandwiches, Brasseries
Average price: €8-20
Area: Centrum
Address: Herengracht 82 1015 BS
Amsterdam The Netherlands
Phone: +31 20 6248195

#183
Blue
Category: Sandwiches, Bar, Cafe
Average price: €8-20
Area: Centrum
Address: Singel 457 1012 WP
Amsterdam The Netherlands
Phone: +31 20 4273901

#184
Studio/K
Category: Dance Club,
Cinema, GastroPub
Average price: €8-20
Area: Oost, Indische Buurt
Address: Timorplein 62 1094 CC
Amsterdam The Netherlands
Phone: +31 20 6920422

#185
Restaurant Shiva
Category: Indian
Average price: €21-40
Area: Centrum
Address: Reguliersdwarsstraat 72-III
1017 BN Amsterdam The Netherlands
Phone: +31 20 6248713

#186
Ethiopisch Eethuis Lalibela
Category: Ethiopian
Average price: €8-20
Area: West, Oud West, Helmersbuurt
Address: Eerste Helmersstraat 249
1054 DX Amsterdam The Netherlands
Phone: +31 20 6838332

#187
Feduzzi's Mercato Italiano
Category: Italian, Delis,
Do-It-Yourself Food
Average price: €8-20
Area: Zuid, Rivierenbuurt
Address: Scheldestraat 63 1078 GH
Amsterdam The Netherlands
Phone: +31 20 6646365

#188
De Pizzabakkers
Category: Italian, Pizza
Average price: €8-20
Area: Zuid, West
Address: Overtoom 501 1054 LH
Amsterdam The Netherlands
Phone: +31 20 6186554

#189
Restaurant Revan
Category: Turkish
Average price: €8-20
Area: Zuid, De Pijp
Address: Van Woustraat 206-212
1073 NA Amsterdam The Netherlands
Phone: +31 20 4700347

#190
De Bakkerswinkel West
Category: Bakeries, Restaurant
Average price: €21-40
Area: West
Address: 1 Polonceaukade 1014 DA
Amsterdam The Netherlands
Phone: +31 20 6880632

#191
Firma Pekelhaaring
Category: Italian
Average price: €21-40
Area: Zuid, De Pijp
Address: Van Woustraat 127-129
1074 AH Amsterdam The Netherlands
Phone: +31 20 6790460

#192
De Italiaan
Category: Italian, Pizza
Average price: €8-20
Area: West, Helmersbuurt
Address: Bosboom Toussaintstraat 29
1054 AN Amsterdam The Netherlands
Phone: +31 20 6836854

#193
Restaurant Jaspers
Category: European
Average price: €21-40
Area: Zuid, De Pijp
Address: Ceintuurbaan 196 1072 GC
Amsterdam The Netherlands
Phone: +31 20 4715233

#194
Japans Restaurant An
Category: Japanese
Average price: €21-40
Area: Centrum
Address: Weteringschans 76 1017 XR
Amsterdam The Netherlands
Phone: +31 20 6244672

#195
Warie's Thai food
Category: Thai
Average price: €8-20
Area: Centrum, Jordaan
Address: Rozengracht 235 1016 NA
Amsterdam The Netherlands
Phone: +31 20 6223638

#196
Struik
Category: Pub, Sandwiches
Average price: Under €7
Area: Centrum, Jordaan
Address: Rozengracht 160 1016 NJ
Amsterdam The Netherlands
Phone: +31 20 6254863

#197
Paso Doble
Category: Tapas
Average price: €8-20
Area: Centrum, Jordaan
Address: Westerstraat 86 1015 MN
Amsterdam The Netherlands
Phone: +31 20 4212670

#198
Novotel Amsterdam
Category: Hotel, Pub, Restaurant
Average price: €8-20
Area: Zuid, Buitenveldert
Address: Europaboulevard 10
1083 AD Amsterdam The Netherlands
Phone: +31 20 5411123

#199
Bistrot Neuf
Category: French
Average price: €21-40
Area: Centrum, Haarlemmerbuurt
Address: Haarlemmerstraat 9
1013 EH Amsterdam The Netherlands
Phone: +31 20 4003210

#200
Restaurant Vapiano
Category: Italian, Bar, Pizza
Average price: €8-20
Area: Centrum
Address: Oosterdokskade 145
1011 DL Amsterdam The Netherlands
Phone: +31 20 4201925

#201
La Rive
Category: Ice Cream, Frozen Yogurt
Average price: €8-20
Area: Plantagebuurt, Centrum
Address: Professor Tupplein 1
1018 GX Amsterdam The Netherlands
Phone: +31 20 520364

#202
Yamazato Restaurant
Category: Japanese
Average price: Above €41
Area: Zuid, De Pijp
Address: Ferdinand Bolstraat 333
1072 LH Amsterdam The Netherlands
Phone: +31 20 6787

#203
Restaurant Vermeer
Category: European
Average price: Above €41
Area: Centrum, De Wallen
Address: Prins Hendrikkade 59 - 72
1012 AD Amsterdam The Netherlands
Phone: +31 20 5564885

#204
't Blauwe Theehuis
Category: GastroPub
Average price: €8-20
Area: Zuid, Museumkwartier
Address: Vondelpark 5 1071 AA
Amsterdam The Netherlands
Phone: +31 20 6620254

#205
Rijsel
Category: French
Average price: €21-40
Area: Oost, Oosterparkbuurt
Address: Marcusstraat 52 B 1091 TK
Amsterdam The Netherlands
Phone: +31 20 4632142

#206
Bella Storia
Category: Italian
Average price: €21-40
Area: West, Staatsliedenbuurt
Address: Bentinckstraat 28 1051 GL
Amsterdam The Netherlands
Phone: +31 20 4880599

#207
Lo Stivale D'oro
Category: Italian
Average price: €8-20
Area: Centrum
Address: Amstelstraat 49 1017 DA
Amsterdam The Netherlands
Phone: +31 20 6387307

#208
Eetcafe Van Beeren
Category: GastroPub, Pub, Brasseries
Average price: €21-40
Area: Centrum
Address: Koningsstraat 54 1011 EW
Amsterdam The Netherlands
Phone: +31 20 6222329

#209
Café Van Leeuwen
Category: GastroPub
Average price: €8-20
Area: Centrum
Address: Keizersgracht 711 1017 DX
Amsterdam The Netherlands
Phone: +31 20 6258215

#210
CAU Carne Argentina Unica
Category: Steakhouses, Argentine
Average price: €21-40
Area: Centrum, De Wallen
Address: Damstraat 5 1012 JL
Amsterdam The Netherlands
Phone: +31 20 6239632

#211
Cotton Cake
Category: Cafe
Average price: €21-40
Area: Zuid, De Pijp
Address: 1e Van Der Helstsrraat 76-hs
1072 NZ Amsterdam The Netherlands
Phone: +31 20 7895838

#212
Blue Pepper Indonesian
Category: Indonesian
Average price: Above €41
Area: West, Helmersbuurt
Address: Nassaukade 366 1054 AB
Amsterdam The Netherlands
Phone: +31 20 4897039

#213
Mashua
Category: Latin American
Average price: €21-40
Area: Centrum
Address: Prinsengracht 703 1017 JV
Amsterdam The Netherlands
Phone: +31 20 4200559

#214
't Vliegertje
Category: GastroPub
Average price: €21-40
Area: Zuid, Rivierenbuurt
Address: Scheldestraat 79 1078 GH
Amsterdam The Netherlands
Phone: +31 20 6798480

#215
Restaurant Fier
Category: Belgian
Average price: €8-20
Area: West, Oud West, Kinkerbuurt
Address: De Clerqstraat 79 1053 AG
Amsterdam The Netherlands
Phone: +31 20 2217449

#216
Caffe Il Momento
Category: Cafe, Coffee & Tea
Average price: €8-20
Area: Centrum
Address: Singel 180 1015 AJ
Amsterdam The Netherlands
Phone: +31 20 3316652

#217
Hoi Tin
Category: Chinese
Average price: €8-20
Area: Centrum, De Wallen
Address: Zeedijk 122-124 1012 BB
Amsterdam The Netherlands
Phone: +31 20 6256451

#218
Pompstation Bar&Grill
Category: Restaurant, Music Venues
Average price: €21-40
Area: Oost, Zeeburg
Address: Zeeburgerdijk 52 1094 AE
Amsterdam The Netherlands
Phone: +31 20 6922888

#219
De Fles
Category: GastroPub
Average price: €8-20
Area: Centrum
Address: Vijzelstraat 137-III 1017 HJ
Amsterdam The Netherlands
Phone: +31 20 6249644

#220
Eetcafe Het Pakhuis
Category: GastroPub
Average price: €8-20
Area: Centrum
Address: Voetboogstraat 10 1012 XL
Amsterdam The Netherlands
Phone: +31 20 6250856

#221
Dauphine Café
Category: Brasseries
Average price: €21-40
Area: Oost, Watergraafsmeer
Address: Prins Bernhardplein 175
1097 BL Amsterdam The Netherlands
Phone: +31 20 4621646

#222
Players Food & Drinks
Category: Pub, Restaurant
Average price: €8-20
Area: Centrum
Address: Kleine Gartmanplantsoen 25
1017 RP Amsterdam The Netherlands
Phone: +31 20 8888886

#223
Stork
Category: Seafood
Average price: €21-40
Area: Noord
Address: Bedrijventerrein de Overkant
1021 KR Amsterdam The Netherlands
Phone: +31 20 6344000

#224
Notting Hill Hotel
Category: Hotel, Nightlife, Restaurant
Average price: Above €41
Area: Centrum
Address: Westeinde 26 1017 ZP
Amsterdam The Netherlands
Phone: +31 20 5231030

#225
Le Fou Fow
Category: Chinese
Average price: €8-20
Area: Centrum, De Wallen
Address: Stormsteeg 9 1012 BD
Amsterdam The Netherlands
Phone: +31 20 2044528

#226
Marius
Category: French
Average price: €21-40
Area: Centrum, West
Address: Barentszstraat 173 1013 NM
Amsterdam The Netherlands
Phone: +31 20 4227880

#227
Nyonya Malasya Express
Category: Malaysian
Average price: €8-20
Area: Centrum, De Wallen
Address: Kloveniersburgwal 38-H
1012 CW Amsterdam The Netherlands
Phone: +31 20 4222447

#228
De Silveren Spiegel
Category: Seafood
Average price: €21-40
Area: Centrum
Address: Kattengat 4-6 1012 SZ
Amsterdam The Netherlands
Phone: +31 20 6246589

#229
Brasserie De Joffers
Category: Brasseries, Diners,
Breakfast & Brunch
Average price: €21-40
Area: Zuid, Museumkwartier
Address: Willemsparkweg 163 1071 GZ
Amsterdam The Netherlands
Phone: +31 20 6730360

#230
Chipsy King
Category: Fish & Chips
Average price: Under €7
Area: Centrum, De Wallen
Address: Damstraat 8 1012 JM
Amsterdam The Netherlands
Phone: +31 624 435003

#231
Café Vrijdag
Category: Cafe
Average price: €8-20
Area: Zuid, Rivierenbuurt
Address: Amsteldijk 137 1079 LE
Amsterdam The Netherlands
Phone: +31 20 7797793

#232
Café Gambrinus
Category: GastroPub, Pub, Dive Bar
Average price: €8-20
Area: Zuid, De Pijp
Address: Ferdinand Bolstraat 180
1072 LV Amsterdam The Netherlands
Phone: +31 20 6717389

#233
Beter & Leuk
Category: Coffee & Tea,
Breakfast & Brunch, GastroPub
Average price: €8-20
Area: Oost, Oosterparkbuurt
Address: Eerste Oosterparkstraat 91
1091 GW Amsterdam The Netherlands
Phone: +31 20 7670029

#234
Kyoto Café
Category: Japanese
Average price: €21-40
Area: Centrum
Address: Damrak 44 1012 LK
Amsterdam The Netherlands
Phone: +31 20 6255302

#235
Bo Cinq
Category: Bar, French, Desserts
Average price: €21-40
Area: Centrum
Address: Prinsengracht 494 1017 KH
Amsterdam The Netherlands
Phone: +31 20 6220682

#236
De Ysbreeker
Category: Cafe, Brasseries, French
Average price: €8-20
Area: Oost, Oosterparkbuurt
Address: Weesperzijde 23 1091 EC
Amsterdam The Netherlands
Phone: +31 20 4681808

#237
Ctaste
Category: Restaurant
Average price: Above €41
Area: Zuid, De Pijp
Address: Amsteldijk 54-55 1074 HX
Amsterdam The Netherlands
Phone: +31 20 6752831

#238
Cafe Restaurant Walem
Category: GastroPub
Average price: €8-20
Area: Centrum
Address: Keizersgracht 449 1017 DK
Amsterdam The Netherlands
Phone: +31 20 6253544

#239
Groot Melkhuis
Category: Breakfast & Brunch
Average price: €8-20
Area: Zuid, Museumkwartier
Address: Vondelpark 2 1071 AA
Amsterdam The Netherlands
Phone: +31 20 6129674

#240
Renzo's
Category: Sandwiches,
Specialty Food, Do-It-Yourself Food
Average price: €8-20
Area: Zuid, Museumkwartier
Address: Van Baerlestraat 67 1071 AR
Amsterdam The Netherlands
Phone: +31 20 6731673

#241
Marathonweg
Category: Cafe, Barbeque
Average price: €21-40
Area: Zuid, Stadionbuurt
Address: Marathonweg 1-3-5 1076 SW
Amsterdam The Netherlands
Phone: +31 20 3703731

#242
Lion Noir
Category: French
Average price: €21-40
Area: Centrum
Address: Reguliersdwarsstraat 28
1017 BM Amsterdam The Netherlands
Phone: +31 20 6276603

#243
Bierfabriek
Category: Barbeque, Pub
Average price: €8-20
Area: Centrum
Address: Rokin 75 1012 KL
Amsterdam The Netherlands
Phone: +31 20 5289910

#244
Wilhelmina-Dok
Category: Mediterranean
Average price: €8-20
Area: Noord
Address: Noordwal 1 1021 PX
Amsterdam The Netherlands
Phone: +31 20 6323701

#245
Japan Inn Yakitori
Category: Sushi Bar, Japanese
Average price: €8-20
Area: Centrum
Address: Leidsekruisstraat 4
1017 RH Amsterdam The Netherlands
Phone: +31 20 6204989

#246
Wagamama
Category: Asian Fusion
Average price: €8-20
Area: Zuid, WTC
Address: Zuidplein 12 1077 XV
Amsterdam The Netherlands
Phone: +31 20 6203032

#247
De Koe
Category: Bar, Cafe
Average price: €8-20
Area: Centrum, Jordaan
Address: Marnixstraat 381 1016 XR
Amsterdam The Netherlands
Phone: +31 20 6254482

#248
Song Kwae Thai Food
Category: Thai
Average price: €8-20
Area: Centrum, De Wallen
Address: Kloveniersburgwal 14-A
1012 CT Amsterdam The Netherlands
Phone: +31 20 6242568

#249
De Waaghals
Category: Vegetarian
Average price: €21-40
Area: Zuid, De Pijp
Address: Frans Halsstraat 29 1072 BK
Amsterdam The Netherlands
Phone: +31 20 6799609

#250
Maurya Organic Indian Lounge
Category: Indian, Specialty Food
Average price: €8-20
Area: Centrum
Address: Korte Leidsedwarsstraat 49A
1017 PW Amsterdam The Netherlands
Phone: +31 20 6263809

#251
Boca's Park
Category: Tapas
Average price: €8-20
Area: Zuid, De Pijp
Address: Sarphatipark 4 1072 PA
Amsterdam The Netherlands
Phone: +31 20 6759945

#252
Café Wheels
Category: Dive Bar, GastroPub
Average price: €8-20
Area: Centrum, Negen Straatjes
Address: Wolvenstraat 4-III 1016 EP
Amsterdam The Netherlands
Phone: +31 20 6228673

#253
The Beef Chief
Category: Burgers
Average price: €8-20
Area: West, Oud West
Address: Jacob van Lennepkade
215 Amsterdam, Noord-Holland
The Netherlands
Phone: +31 619 997846

#254
Sari Citra
Category: Indonesian
Average price: Under €7
Area: Zuid, De Pijp
Address: Ferdinand Bolstraat 52
1072 LL Amsterdam The Netherlands
Phone: +31 20 6754102

#255
Daalder
Category: GastroPub
Average price: €8-20
Area: Centrum, Jordaan
Address: Lindengracht 90 1015 KK
Amsterdam The Netherlands
Phone: +31 20 6248864

#256
Yokiyo
Category: Korean
Average price: €21-40
Area: Centrum, De Wallen
Address: Oudezijds Voorburgwal 67
1012 EK Amsterdam The Netherlands
Phone: +31 20 3314562

#257
Pink Flamingo Pizza
Category: Pizza
Average price: €8-20
Area: Zuid, De Pijp
Address: Gerard Douplein 8 1072 VE
Amsterdam The Netherlands
Phone: +31 20 6703274

#258
Ron Gastrobar
Category: French, GastroPub
Average price: Above €41
Area: Zuid, Willemspark
Address: Sophialaan 55 1075 BP
Amsterdam The Netherlands
Phone: +31 20 4961943

#259
Tokyo Cafe
Category: Japanese, Sushi Bar
Average price: €21-40
Area: Centrum
Address: Spui 15 1012 WX
Amsterdam The Netherlands
Phone: +31 20 4897918

#260
Meuwese Espresso
Category: Coffee & Tea, Brasseries
Average price: €8-20
Area: Centrum, De Wallen
Address: Rokin 119 1012 KP
Amsterdam The Netherlands
Phone: +31 20 6241243

#261
Sonny
Category: Falafel, Vegan, Vegetarian
Average price: Under €7
Area: Zuid, De Pijp
Address: Eerste van der Helststraat 43
1073 AC Amsterdam The Netherlands
Phone: +31 20 6767612

#262
Olijfje
Category: Mediterranean
Average price: €8-20
Area: Centrum
Address: Valkenburgerstraat 223-D
1011 MJ Amsterdam The Netherlands
Phone: +31 20 3304444

#263
Gebr.
Category: Cafe
Average price: Above €41
Area: Centrum
Address: Peperstraat 10hs 1011 NX
'Amsterdam The Netherlands
Phone: +31 20 4210699

#264
Surya
Category: Indian, Vegetarian
Average price: €21-40
Area: Zuid, De Pijp
Address: Ceintuurbaan 147 1072 GB
Amsterdam The Netherlands
Phone: +31 20 6767985

#265
Screaming Beans
Category: Pub, Wine Bar
Average price: €21-40
Area: West, Oud West, Helmersbuurt
Address: Eerste Constantijn Huygensstraat
35 1054 BR Amsterdam The Netherlands
Phone: +31 20 6160770

#266
Dragon i
Category: Japanese, Korean, Thai
Average price: €8-20
Area: Zuid
Address: Amstelveenseweg 154
1075 XM Amsterdam The Netherlands
Phone: +31 20 7706420

#267
Belgisch Restaurant Lieve Amsterdam
Category: Belgian
Average price: €8-20
Area: Centrum
Address: Herengracht 88 1015 BS
Amsterdam The Netherlands
Phone: +31 20 6249635

#268
De Duvel Eetcafé
Category: GastroPub
Average price: €8-20
Area: Zuid, De Pijp
Address: 1e van der Helststraat 59-HS
1073 AD Amsterdam The Netherlands
Phone: +31 20 6757517

#269
Kam Yin
Category: Chinese, Indonesian
Average price: €8-20
Area: Centrum, De Wallen
Address: Warmoesstraat 6 1012 JD
Amsterdam The Netherlands
Phone: +31 20 6253115

#270
BAUT Amsterdam
Category: French,
Juice Bar & Smoothies, Italian
Average price: €21-40
Area: Oost, Oosterparkbuurt
Address: Wibautstraat 125 1091 GL
Amsterdam The Netherlands
Phone: +31 20 4659260

#271
Pilsvogel
Category: GastroPub, Tapas
Average price: €8-20
Area: Zuid, De Pijp
Address: Gerard Douplein 14
1072 VE Amsterdam The Netherlands
Phone: +31 20 6646483

#272
Bagels & Beans
Category: Bagels, Coffee & Tea,
Gluten-Free
Average price: €8-20
Area: Zuid, De Pijp
Address: Ferdinand Bolstraat 70
1072 LM Amsterdam The Netherlands
Phone: +31 20 6721610

#273
Dwaze Zaken
Category: Do-It-Yourself Food,
Cafe, Brasseries
Average price: €8-20
Area: Centrum, De Wallen
Address: Prins Hendrikkade 50
1012 AC Amsterdam The Netherlands
Phone: +31 20 6124175

#274
Balraj
Category: Indian
Average price: €8-20
Area: Centrum, Haarlemmerbuurt
Address: Haarlemmerdijk 28-II
1013 JD Amsterdam The Netherlands
Phone: +31 20 6251428

#275
China Sichuan
Category: Chinese
Average price: €21-40
Area: Centrum, De Wallen
Address: Warmoesstraat 17
1012 HT Amsterdam The Netherlands
Phone: +31 20 4207833

#276
Oliver's
Category: European
Average price: €8-20
Area: Zuid, WTC
Address: Claude Debussylaan 78
1082 MD Amsterdam The Netherlands
Phone: +31 20 6461626

#277
Zouk
Category: GastroPub, Pub
Average price: €8-20
Area: West, Oud West, Helmersbuurt
Address: 1e C Huygensstr 45 1054 BS
Amsterdam The Netherlands
Phone: +31 20 6891133

#278
Thai Tiger
Category: Thai
Average price: €8-20
Area: Oost, Indische Buurt
Address: Javaplein 7a 1095 CH
Amsterdam The Netherlands
Phone: +31 20 2210858

#279
Fuoco Vivo
Category: Pizza
Average price: €8-20
Area: West, Da Costabuurt
Address: De Clercqstraat 12-BG 1052 NC
Amsterdam The Netherlands
Phone: +31 20 6124309

#280
NH Grand Hotel Krasnapolsky
Category: Hotel, Restaurant
Average price: €21-40
Area: Centrum, De Wallen
Address: Dam 9 1012 JS
Amsterdam The Netherlands
Phone: +31 20 5549111

#281
Bickers Aan De Werf
Category: Salad, Sandwiches
Average price: €21-40
Area: Centrum, Haarlemmerbuurt
Address: Bickerswerf 2 1013 KX
Amsterdam The Netherlands
Phone: +31 20 3202951

#282
Sazanka Restaurant
Category: Japanese
Average price: Above €41
Area: Zuid, De Pijp
Address: Ferdinand Bolstraat 333
1072 LH Amsterdam The Netherlands
Phone: +31 20 6787111

#283
Koffiehuis Van Den Volksbond
Category: GastroPub
Average price: €8-20
Area: Centrum
Address: Kadijksplein 4 1018 AB
Amsterdam The Netherlands
Phone: +31 20 6221209

#284
Gare de l'Est
Category: French
Average price: €21-40
Area: Oost, Zeeburg
Address: Cruqiusweg 9 1019 AT
Amsterdam The Netherlands
Phone: +31 20 4630620

#285
CrepeBar
Category: Creperies, Cafe
Average price: €8-20
Area: Centrum
Address: Martelaarsgracht 11
1012 TN Amsterdam The Netherlands
Phone: +31 20 4896262

#286
Kaiko
Category: Sushi Bar
Average price: Above €41
Area: Zuid, Rivierenbuurt
Address: Jekerstraat 114 1078 MJ
Amsterdam The Netherlands
Phone: +31 20 6625641

#287
Hugo's Bar & Kitchen
Category: Restaurant, Cocktail Bar
Average price: €8-20
Area: West, Frederik Hendrikbuurt
Address: Hugo de Grootplein 10 1052 KW
Amsterdam The Netherlands
Phone: +31 20 7516633

#288
Japans Delicatessenhuis Zen
Category: Japanese, Diners
Average price: €21-40
Area: Zuid, De Pijp
Address: Frans Halsstraat 38 1072 BS
Amsterdam The Netherlands
Phone: +31 20 6270607

#289
The Lobby
Category: European
Average price: Above €41
Area: Centrum, De Wallen
Address: Nes 49 1012 KD
Amsterdam The Netherlands
Phone: +31 20 7585275

#290
Renato's Pizzeria
Category: Pizza, Italian
Average price: €21-40
Area: Zuid, De Pijp
Address: Karel du Jardinstraat 32
1072 SK Amsterdam The Netherlands
Phone: +31 20 6732300

#291
Sefa Grill-Shoarma
Category: Fast Food, Diners, Turkish
Average price: €8-20
Area: Centrum
Address: Westermarkt 25 1016 DJ
Amsterdam The Netherlands
Phone: +31 20 7739212

#292
Me Naam Naan
Category: Thai
Average price: €21-40
Area: Centrum
Address: Koningsstraat 29 1011 ET
Amsterdam The Netherlands
Phone: +31 20 4233344

#293
Comfort Caffè
Category: Italian
Average price: €21-40
Area: Oost, Indische Buurt
Address: Sumatrastraat 28-30
1094 ND Amsterdam The Netherlands
Phone: +31 20 4630092

#294
Cafe Sonneveld
Category: Cafe
Average price: €8-20
Area: Centrum, Jordaan
Address: Egelantiersgracht 72-74
1015 RN Amsterdam The Netherlands
Phone: +31 20 4234287

#295
Spanjer En Van Twist
Category: GastroPub
Average price: €8-20
Area: Centrum
Address: Leliegracht 60 1015 DJ
Amsterdam The Netherlands
Phone: +31 20 6390109

#296
Le Pain Quotidien Oud Zuid
Category: Belgian,
Breakfast & Brunch, Sandwiches
Average price: €8-20
Area: Zuid, Museumkwartier
Address: Johannes Verhulststraat 104
1071 NL Amsterdam The Netherlands
Phone: +31 20 3795900

#297
Sushi Me
Category: Sushi Bar
Average price: €8-20
Area: Centrum
Address: Oude Leliestraat 7-BG 1016 BD
Amsterdam The Netherlands
Phone: +31 20 6277043

#298
Restaurant Bidou
Category: French, Italian
Average price: €21-40
Area: Oost, Oosterparkbuurt
Address: Beukenplein 19-21 1092 BB
Amsterdam The Netherlands
Phone: +31 20 3624390

#299
Pizza Sotto
Category: Pizza
Average price: €8-20
Area: Zuid, Willemspark
Address: Amstelveenseweg 89 1075 VW
Amsterdam The Netherlands
Phone: +31 20 2239000

#300
Café Schiller
Category: Cafe, Brasseries
Average price: €8-20
Area: Centrum
Address: Rembrandtplein 24 1017 CV
Amsterdam The Netherlands
Phone: +31 20 6249846

#301
De Smoeshaan
Category: Pub, GastroPub
Average price: €8-20
Area: West
Address: Leidsekade 90 1017 PN
Amsterdam The Netherlands
Phone: +31 20 6250368

#302
Febo
Category: Fast Food
Average price: Under €7
Area: Centrum
Address: Reguliersbreestraat 38
1017 CN Amsterdam The Netherlands
Phone: +31 20 6235304

#303
Vlaming
Category: GastroPub
Average price: €21-40
Area: Centrum, Jordaan
Address: Lindengracht 95 1015 KD
Amsterdam The Netherlands
Phone: +31 20 6222716

#304
Restaurant Chang-I
Category: Asian Fusion
Average price: €8-20
Area: Zuid, Museumkwartier
Address: Jan Willem Brouwersstr 7
1071 LH Amsterdam The Netherlands
Phone: +31 20 4701700

#305
Spare Rib Express
Category: Barbeque, Steakhouses
Average price: €8-20
Area: Oost, Zeeburg
Address: Veemarkt 76 1019 DD
Amsterdam The Netherlands
Phone: +31 20 4687647

#306
Na Siam
Category: Thai
Average price: €8-20
Area: Centrum
Address: Kerkstraat 332 1017 JA
Amsterdam The Netherlands
Phone: +31 20 4210505

#307
Maoz Falafel
Category: Vegetarian
Average price: Under €7
Area: Centrum
Address: Muntplein 1 1017 CM
Amsterdam The Netherlands
Phone: +31 20 6249290

#308
La Perla
Category: Pizza, Italian
Average price: €8-20
Area: Centrum, Jordaan
Address: Tweede Tuindwarsstraat 14,
Amsterdam The Netherlands
Phone: +31 20 6876230

#309
Bar Baarsch
Category: GastroPub
Average price: €8-20
Area: West, Hoofdweg en Omgeving
Address: Jan Evertsenstraat 91 1057 BS
Amsterdam The Netherlands
Phone: +31 20 6181970

#310
NAM KEE
Category: Chinese
Average price: €8-20
Area: Centrum, De Wallen
Address: Zeedijk 111-113 1012 AV
Amsterdam The Netherlands
Phone: +31 20 6243470

#311
Café Thuys
Category: Pub, Food
Average price: €8-20
Area: West, Oud West, Kinkerbuurt
Address: De Clercqstraat 129 1053 AK
Amsterdam The Netherlands
Phone: +31 20 6120898

#312
Casa Di David
Category: Italian
Average price: €8-20
Area: Centrum
Address: Singel 426-BG 1017 AV
Amsterdam The Netherlands
Phone: +31 20 6262429

#313
O'reilly's
Category: Pub, GastroPub, Irish
Average price: €8-20
Area: Centrum
Address: Paleisstraat 103-105
1012 ZL Amsterdam The Netherlands
Phone: +31 20 6249498

#314
Nooch
Category: Asian Fusion
Average price: €8-20
Area: Centrum, Negen Straatjes
Address: Reestraat 11 1016 DM
Amsterdam The Netherlands
Phone: +31 20 6222105

#315
Barça
Category: Spanish, Pub, Tapas Bar
Average price: €8-20
Area: Zuid, De Pijp
Address: Marie Heinekenplein 30-31
1072 MH Amsterdam The Netherlands
Phone: +31 20 4704144

#316
Pompa
Category: Italian
Average price: €8-20
Area: Zuid, Museumkwartier
Address: Willemsparkweg 6 1071 HD
Amsterdam The Netherlands
Phone: +31 20 6626206

#317
Gollem's Proeflokaal
Category: Pub, GastroPub
Average price: €8-20
Area: West, Oud West, Helmersbuurt
Address: Overtoom 160-162 1054 HP
Amsterdam The Netherlands
Phone: +31 20 6129444

#318
Café Maxwell
Category: GastroPub
Average price: €8-20
Area: Oost, Oosterparkbuurt
Address: Beukenplein 27 1092 BB
Amsterdam The Netherlands
Phone: +31 20 7726748

#319
Pizzeria San Marco
Category: Do-It-Yourself Food, Italian
Average price: €8-20
Area: Zuid, De Pijp
Address: Amstelkade 148-A 1078 AW
Amsterdam The Netherlands
Phone: +31 20 6730884

#320
Eye Bar & Restaurant
Category: GastroPub
Average price: €8-20
Area: Noord
Address: IJpromenade 1 1031 KT
Amsterdam The Netherlands
Phone: +31 20 5891402

#321
Bagels & Beans
Category: Bagels, Coffee & Tea,
Breakfast & Brunch
Average price: €8-20
Area: Centrum
Address: Waterlooplein 2 1011 PG
Amsterdam The Netherlands
Phone: +31 20 4288906

#322
Izakaya
Category: Japanese, Asian Fusion
Average price: Above €41
Area: Zuid, De Pijp
Address: Albert Cuypstraat 2-6
1072 CT Amsterdam The Netherlands
Phone: +31 20 3053090

#323
Café De Blauwe Pan
Category: GastroPub
Average price: Under €7
Area: Centrum, Jordaan
Address: Westerstraat 200
1015 MS Amsterdam The Netherlands
Phone: +31 20 3207211

#324
Café Flinck
Category: GastroPub, Pub
Average price: €8-20
Area: Zuid, De Pijp
Address: 1e van der Helststraat 51
1073 AD Amsterdam The Netherlands
Phone: +31 20 8462101

#325
Momo
Category: Asian Fusion
Average price: €21-40
Area: Zuid, Museumkwartier
Address: Hobbemastraat 1 1071 XZ
Amsterdam The Netherlands
Phone: +31 20 6717474

#326
Café Kobalt
Category: GastroPub, Pub
Average price: €8-20
Area: Centrum, Haarlemmerbuurt
Address: Singel 2-A 1013 GA
Amsterdam The Netherlands
Phone: +31 20 3201959

#327
Loetje Oost
Category: Salad, Sandwiches
Average price: €21-40
Area: Oost, Oosterparkbuurt
Address: Ruyschstraat 15 1091 BR
Amsterdam The Netherlands
Phone: +31 20 3624709

#328
Sushi Time
Category: Japanese
Average price: €8-20
Area: Zuid, WTC
Address: Strawinskylaan 13
1077 XW Amsterdam The Netherlands
Phone: +31 20 5753200

#329
Spijshuys Versch
Category: Restaurant
Average price: €8-20
Area: Zuid, Museumkwartier
Address: Ruysdaelkade 183
1072 AT Amsterdam The Netherlands
Phone: +31 611 628545

#330
Cut Throat Barber & Coffee
Category: Barbers, Coffee & Tea
Average price: €21-40
Area: Centrum, De Wallen
Address: Warmoesstraat 155
1012 JC Amsterdam The Netherlands
Phone: +31 625 343769

#331
De Kaasboer
Category: Food, Sandwiches
Average price: Under €7
Area: Centrum, Jordaan
Address: Tweede Tuindwarsstraat 3
1015 RX Amsterdam The Netherlands
Phone: +31 20 6248802

#332
Betty's
Category: Vegetarian
Average price: €21-40
Area: Zuid, Rivierenbuurt
Address: Rijnstraat 75-HS 1079 GX
Amsterdam The Netherlands
Phone: +31 20 6445896

#333
Sane
Category: Do-It-Yourself Food,
Juice Bar & Smoothies, Soup
Average price: Under €7
Area: Centrum, Haarlemmerbuurt
Address: Haarlemmerdijk 136
1013 JJ Amsterdam The Netherlands
Phone: +31 20 2237211

#334
Serre Restaurant
Category: French, European
Average price: €21-40
Area: Zuid, De Pijp
Address: Ferdinand Bolstraat 333
1072 LH Amsterdam The Netherlands
Phone: +31 20 6787450

#335
The Burrito Maker
Category: Tex-Mex
Average price: €8-20
Area: Centrum, Haarlemmerbuurt
Address: Haarlemmerplein 29 1013 HP
Amsterdam The Netherlands
Phone: +31 20 4208383

#336
Yam Yam Trattoria - Pizzeria
Category: Italian
Average price: €8-20
Area: West, Frederik Hendrikbuurt
Address: Frederik Hendrikstraat 90
1052 HZ Amsterdam The Netherlands
Phone: +31 20 6815097

#337
Ponte Arcari
Category: Italian
Average price: €21-40
Area: Centrum
Address: Herengracht 534 1017 CG
Amsterdam The Netherlands
Phone: +31 20 6250853

#338
Lucius Visrestaurant
Category: Fish & Chips
Average price: €21-40
Area: Centrum
Address: Spuistraat 247 1012 VP
Amsterdam The Netherlands
Phone: +31 20 6241831

#339
College Hotel
Category: Lounge, Hotel
Average price: €21-40
Area: Zuid, Museumkwartier
Address: Roelof Hartstraat 1
1071 VE Amsterdam The Netherlands
Phone: +31 20 5711511

#340
Sumo Sushi & Grill
Category: Japanese
Average price: €8-20
Area: Centrum
Address: Vijzelstraat 26 1017 HK
Amsterdam The Netherlands
Phone: +31 20 4207822

#341
Hemelse Modder
Category: European
Average price: €21-40
Area: Centrum
Address: Oude Waal 11 1011 BZ
Amsterdam The Netherlands
Phone: +31 20 6243203

#342
Tibet Restaurant
Category: Soup
Average price: €8-20
Area: Centrum, De Wallen
Address: Lange Niezel 24 1012 GT
Amsterdam The Netherlands
Phone: +31 20 6241137

#343
Restaurant Dubbel
Category: GastroPub
Average price: €8-20
Area: Centrum
Address: Lijnbaansgracht 256
1017 RK Amsterdam The Netherlands
Phone: +31 20 6200909

#344
Ko Chang
Category: Thai
Average price: €8-20
Area: Centrum, Jordaan
Address: Westerstraat 91 1015 LX
Amsterdam The Netherlands
Phone: +31 20 6381039

#345
Frederique
Category: Specialty Food,
Sandwiches, Salad
Average price: Under €7
Area: Zuid, De Pijp
Address: Gerard Doustraat 224
1073 XC Amsterdam The Netherlands
Phone: +31 20 7740332

#346
Restaurant Spelt
Category: European,
Breakfast & Brunch
Average price: €21-40
Area: Centrum
Address: Nieuwe Spiegelstraat 5a
1017 DB Amsterdam The Netherlands
Phone: +31 20 4207022

#347
**Holland International
Canal Cruises**
Category: Nightlife,
Arts & Entertainment
Average price: €8-20
Area: Centrum
Address: Prins Hendrikkade 33a
1012 TM Amsterdam The Netherlands
Phone: +31 20 6253035

#348
Stoop & Stoop Eetcafé
Category: GastroPub
Average price: €8-20
Area: Centrum
Address: Lange Leidsedwarsstraat
82-HS 1017 NM Amsterdam
The Netherlands
Phone: +31 20 6200982

#349
Ciro Passami L'olio!
Category: Italian
Average price: Above €41
Area: West, Helmersbuurt
Address: Tweede Helmersstraat 3-BG
1054 CA Amsterdam The Netherlands
Phone: +31 615 699649

#350
Brasserie Blazer
Category: Brasseries
Average price: €8-20
Area: Centrum, Jordaan
Address: Lijnbaansgracht 190
1016 XA Amsterdam The Netherlands
Phone: +31 20 6209690

#351
Wijnbar Boelen & Boelen
Category: French, Wine Bar
Average price: €8-20
Area: Zuid, De Pijp
Address: 1e van der Helststraat 50
1072 NV Amsterdam The Netherlands
Phone: +31 20 6712242

#352
Dante Kitchen & Bar
Category: Pub, Italian
Average price: €8-20
Area: Centrum
Address: Spuistraat 320 1012 VX
Amsterdam The Netherlands
Phone: +31 20 6246266

#353
Ristorante Saturnino
Category: Italian
Average price: €21-40
Area: Centrum
Address: Reguliersdwarsstraat 3-5
1017 BJ Amsterdam The Netherlands
Phone: +31 20 6390102

#354
Khorat Top Thai
Category: Thai, Food Delivery Services
Average price: €8-20
Area: West, Oud West
Address: 2de C. Huygensstraat 64
Amsterdam, Noord-Holland
The Netherlands
Phone: +31 20 6831297

#355
Espressobar Puccini
Category: Coffee & Tea, Brasseries
Average price: €21-40
Area: Centrum
Address: Staalstraat 21 1011 JK
Amsterdam The Netherlands
Phone: +31 20 6208458

#356
Max
Category: French, Indonesian
Average price: €21-40
Area: Centrum
Address: Herenstraat 14 1015 CA
Amsterdam The Netherlands
Phone: +31 20 4200222

#357
Restaurant Caprese
Category: Italian
Average price: €8-20
Area: Centrum
Address: Spuistraat 261 1012 VR
Amsterdam The Netherlands
Phone: +31 20 6200059

#358
Lunchcafé Studio 2
Category: GastroPub
Average price: €8-20
Area: Centrum
Address: Singel 504 1017 AX
Amsterdam The Netherlands
Phone: +31 20 6239136

#359
CC Muziekcafé
Category: Jazz & Blues,
Music Venues, Cafe
Average price: Under €7
Area: Zuid, De Pijp
Address: Rustenburgerstraat 384
1072 HG Amsterdam The Netherlands
Phone: +31 624 236956

#360
Van Speyk
Category: Brasseries
Average price: €21-40
Area: Centrum
Address: Spuistraat 3a 1012 SP
Amsterdam The Netherlands
Phone: +31 20 4200117

#361
Pastis
Category: European
Average price: €8-20
Area: West, Oud West, Helmersbuurt
Address: 1e Constantijn Huygenstraat 15
1054 BP Amsterdam The Netherlands
Phone: +31 20 6166166

#362
Febo
Category: Fast Food
Average price: Under €7
Area: Centrum
Address: Leidsestraat 121 1017 NZ
Amsterdam The Netherlands
Phone: +31 20 4343556

#363
Caffe Milo
Category: Pub, Italian, GastroPub
Average price: €8-20
Area: Oost, Dapperbuurt
Address: Linnaeusstraat 71-H
1093 EJ Amsterdam The Netherlands
Phone: +31 20 4638027

#364
De Wasserette
Category: Sandwiches, Coffee & Tea
Average price: €8-20
Area: Zuid, De Pijp
Address: Eerste van der Helststraat 27
1073 AC Oud-Zuid
The Netherlands
Phone: +31 20 4638027

#365
Drovers Dog
Category: Do-It-Yourself Food,
Coffee & Tea, Australian
Average price: €8-20
Area: Oost, Indische Buurt
Address: Eerste Atjehstraat 62
1094 KP Amsterdam The Netherlands
Phone: +31 20 3703784

#366
Toastable
Category: Breakfast & Brunch,
Juice Bar & Smoothies, Cafe
Average price: €8-20
Area: Centrum
Address: Singel 441 Sous 1012 WP
Amsterdam The Netherlands
Phone: +31 20 6262969

#367
Maoz Falafel
Category: Fast Food
Average price: Under €7
Area: Centrum
Address: Leidsestraat 85 1017 NX
Amsterdam The Netherlands
Phone: +31 20 4279720

#368
Hostaria
Category: Italian
Average price: €8-20
Area: Centrum, Jordaan
Address: 2e Egelantiersdwarsstraat 9
1015 SB Amsterdam The Netherlands
Phone: +31 20 6260028

#369
Café De Engelbewaarder
Category: Pub, GastroPub
Average price: €8-20
Area: Centrum
Address: Kloveniersburgwal 59-HS
1011 JZ Amsterdam The Netherlands
Phone: +31 20 6253772

#370
@ Seven
Category: Breakfast & Brunch
Average price: €8-20
Area: Zuid, Rivierenbuurt
Address: Scheldestraat 92 1078 GN
Amsterdam The Netherlands
Phone: +31 20 6709295

#371
Getto
Category: Gay Bar, GastroPub
Average price: €8-20
Area: Centrum, De Wallen
Address: Warmoesstraat 51-B
1012 HW Amsterdam The Netherlands
Phone: +31 20 4215151

#372
Café Restaurant Kapitein Zeppos
Category: Diners, Pub
Average price: €8-20
Area: Centrum, De Wallen
Address: Gebed Zonder End 5
1012 HS Amsterdam The Netherlands
Phone: +31 20 6242057

#373
Mazzo
Category: Beer, Wine & Spirits
Average price: €8-20
Area: Centrum, Jordaan
Address: Rozengracht 114 1016 NH
Amsterdam The Netherlands
Phone: +31 20 3446402

#374
Cafe Nassau
Category: Italian
Average price: €8-20
Area: West, Staatsliedenbuurt
Address: De Wittenkade 105-A
1052 AG Amsterdam The Netherlands
Phone: +31 20 6843562

#375
Charles Eten & Drinken
Category: Salad, Sandwiches
Average price: €8-20
Area: Oost, Oosterparkbuurt
Address: Linnaeuskade 3 1098 BC
Amsterdam The Netherlands
Phone: +31 20 6634359

#376
Think Soup
Category: Cafe, Soup
Average price: Under €7
Area: Centrum, Jordaan
Address: Kinkerstraat 83hs 1053 DH
Amsterdam The Netherlands
Phone: +31 20 2332150

#377
Wurst & Schnitzelhaus
Category: German
Average price: €8-20
Area: Centrum
Address: Prinsengracht 474 hs
1017 KG Amsterdam The Netherlands
Phone: +31 20 7371592

#378
Madrid
Category: Tapas Bar, Spanish
Average price: €8-20
Area: West, Oud West, Kinkerbuurt
Address: Bellamystraat 11 1053 BM
Amsterdam The Netherlands
Phone: +31 20 4899375

#379
De Pizzakamer
Category: Pizza
Average price: €8-20
Area: Zuid, De Pijp
Address: 2e van der Helststraat 16
1072 PD Amsterdam The Netherlands
Phone: +31 20 2211457

#380
Otaru
Category: Japanese
Average price: €8-20
Area: Zuid, De Pijp
Address: Frans Halsstraat 2 1072 BR
Amsterdam The Netherlands
Phone: +31 20 6708972

#381
LAB111
Category: Diners, Cafe
Average price: €8-20
Area: West, Oud West, Helmersbuurt
Address: Arie Biemondstraat 111 1054 PD
Amsterdam The Netherlands
Phone: +31 20 6169994

#382
Nel
Category: Desserts, Diners, Cafe
Average price: €8-20
Area: Centrum
Address: Amstelveld 12 1017 JD
Amsterdam The Netherlands
Phone: +31 20 6261199

#383
Vapiano Rembrandtplein
Category: Italian, Mediterranean
Average price: €8-20
Area: Centrum
Address: Amstelstraat 2-4 1017 DA
Amsterdam The Netherlands
Phone: +31 20 7670800

#384
Humphrey's
Category: Brasseries
Average price: €21-40
Area: Centrum
Address: Nieuwezijds Kolk 23 1012 PV
Amsterdam The Netherlands
Phone: +31 20 4221234

#385
't Fornuis
Category: French
Average price: €21-40
Area: Centrum
Address: Utrechtsestraat 33 1017 VH
Amsterdam The Netherlands
Phone: +31 20 6269139

#386
Sapporo
Category: Japanese
Average price: Above €41
Area: Zuid, Rivierenbuurt
Address: Scheldestraat 99 1078 GJ
Amsterdam The Netherlands
Phone: +31 20 4710039

#387
Kobe House
Category: Japanese
Average price: €21-40
Area: Centrum
Address: Nieuwezijds Voorburgwal 77
1012 RE Amsterdam The Netherlands
Phone: +31 20 6226458

#388
Golden Brown Bar
Category: GastroPub, Bar, Thai
Average price: €8-20
Area: West, Oud West, Helmersbuurt
Address: Jan Pieter Heijestraat 146
1054 WT Amsterdam The Netherlands
Phone: +31 20 6124076

#389
Het Bosch
Category: Lounge, Seafood, French
Average price: €21-40
Area: Zuid, Buitenveldert
Address: Jollenpad 10 1081 KC
Amsterdam The Netherlands
Phone: +31 20 6445800

#390
Restaurant Luna
Category: Argentine,
Steakhouses, Latin American
Average price: €21-40
Area: Centrum, Jordaan
Address: Lindengracht 152 1015 KK
Amsterdam The Netherlands
Phone: +31 20 6274149

#391
Los Pilones
Category: Mexican
Average price: €8-20
Area: Centrum, De Wallen
Address: Geldersekade 111 1011 EN
Amsterdam The Netherlands
Phone: +31 20 7760210

#392
Thaicoon
Category: Thai
Average price: €8-20
Area: Oost, Oosterparkbuurt
Address: Beukenplein 10 1091 KG
Amsterdam The Netherlands
Phone: +31 20 3623302

#393
Dos
Category: Tapas Bar, Spanish
Average price: €21-40
Area: Centrum, Jordaan
Address: Nieuwe Willemsstraat 1
1015 JH Amsterdam The Netherlands
Phone: +31 620 429303

#394
Assaggi
Category: Italian
Average price: €8-20
Area: Centrum, Jordaan
Address: Tweede Egelantiersdwstr 4-6
1015 SC Amsterdam The Netherlands
Phone: +31 20 4205589

#395
Café de Gaeper
Category: Pub, GastroPub
Average price: €8-20
Area: Centrum
Address: Staalstraat 4-IV 1011 JL
Amsterdam The Netherlands
Phone: +31 20 6233895

#396
Louter
Category: Brasseries
Average price: €8-20
Area: West, Oud West, Da Costabuurt
Address: De Clercqstraat 82 1052 NK
Amsterdam The Netherlands
Phone: +31 20 3892623

#397
Casa Peru
Category: Peruvian
Average price: €21-40
Area: Centrum
Address: Leidsegracht 68-SOUS
1016 CP Amsterdam The Netherlands
Phone: +31 20 6203749

#398
Bosco
Category: GastroPub
Average price: €8-20
Area: West, Oud West, Helmersbuurt
Address: Eerste Constantijn Huygensstraat
7-9 1054 BN Amsterdam The Netherlands
Phone: +31 20 2213480

#399
Nomads
Category: Middle Eastern, Hookah Bar
Average price: €21-40
Area: Centrum, Jordaan
Address: Rozengracht 133 I 1016 LV
Amsterdam The Netherlands
Phone: +31 20 3446405

#400
Tasca Bellota
Category: Tapas, Spanish
Average price: €8-20
Area: Centrum
Address: Herenstraat 22 1015 CB
Amsterdam The Netherlands
Phone: +31 20 4202946

#401
Bistro Bonjour
Category: French
Average price: €8-20
Area: Centrum
Address: Keizersgracht 770 1017 EB
Amsterdam The Netherlands
Phone: +31 20 6266040

#402
Sa Seada
Category: Italian
Average price: €8-20
Area: Oost, Oosterparkbuurt
Address: Eerste Oosterparkstraat 3-5
1091 GT Amsterdam The Netherlands
Phone: +31 20 6633276

#403
Kok Kita
Category: Indonesian,
Do-It-Yourself Food
Average price: Under €7
Area: Zuid
Address: Amstelveenseweg 166
1075 XN Amsterdam The Netherlands
Phone: +31 20 6702933

#404
A la Ferme
Category: French
Average price: €8-20
Area: Zuid, De Pijp
Address: Govert Flinckstraat 251
1073 BX Amsterdam The Netherlands
Phone: +31 20 6798240

#405
Hutspot
Category: Cafe
Average price: Under €7
Area: Centrum, Jordaan
Address: Rozengracht 204-210
1016 NL Amsterdam The Netherlands
Phone: +31 20 2231331

#406
Terang Boelan Afhaalcentrum
Category: Indonesian
Average price: €8-20
Area: Centrum, Jordaan
Address: Tweede Lindendwarsstraat
3-HS 1015 LH Amsterdam The Netherlands
Phone: +31 20 6209974

#407
Daarbaand
Category: Persian/Iranian
Average price: €8-20
Area: West, Oud West, Helmersbuurt
Address: Overtoom 350 1054 JG
Amsterdam The Netherlands
Phone: +31 20 6185481

#408
De Ebeling
Category: Bar, GastroPub
Average price: €8-20
Area: West, Helmersbuurt
Address: Overtoom 50-54 1054 HK
Amsterdam The Netherlands
Phone: +31 20 6891218

#409
De Blauwe Engel
Category: GastroPub
Average price: €8-20
Area: Zuid, WTC
Address: Strawinskylaan 143 1077 XX
Amsterdam The Netherlands
Phone: +31 20 5752140

#410
Café Restaurant Van Puffelen
Category: Restaurant
Average price: €8-20
Area: Centrum, Negen Straatjes
Address: Prinsengracht 375-HS
1016 HL Amsterdam The Netherlands
Phone: +31 20 6246270

#411
Café de Doelen
Category: Pub, GastroPub
Average price: €8-20
Area: Centrum
Address: Kloveniersburgwal 125
1011 KC Amsterdam The Netherlands
Phone: +31 20 6249023

#412
Stacey's Pennywell
Category: GastroPub
Average price: €8-20
Area: Centrum
Address: Herengracht 558 1017 CG
Amsterdam The Netherlands
Phone: +31 20 6243506

#413
Bark
Category: Brasseries, Seafood, French
Average price: €21-40
Area: Zuid, Museumkwartier
Address: Van Baerlestraat 120 1071 BD
Amsterdam The Netherlands
Phone: +31 20 6750210

#414
Goodies
Category: Cafe
Average price: €8-20
Area: Centrum, Negen Straatjes
Address: Huidenstraat 9 1016 ER
Amsterdam The Netherlands
Phone: +31 20 6256122

#415
Bar Bukowski
Category: Cafe, Breakfast & Brunch
Average price: €8-20
Area: Oost, Oosterparkbuurt
Address: Oosterpark 10 1092 AE
Amsterdam The Netherlands
Phone: +31 20 6654893

#416
Febo
Category: Fast Food
Average price: Under €7
Area: Centrum
Address: Nieuwendijk 220 1012 MX
Amsterdam The Netherlands
Phone: +31 20 6259906

#417
Sea Palace
Category: Chinese
Average price: €8-20
Area: Centrum
Address: Oosterdokskade 8 1011 AE
Amsterdam The Netherlands
Phone: +31 20 6258672

#418
Bar Lempicka
Category: Brasseries, Cocktail Bar
Average price: €8-20
Area: Plantagebuurt, Centrum
Address: Sarphatistraat 23 1018 EV
Amsterdam The Netherlands
Phone: +31 20 6220209

#419
Café Het Molenpad
Category: GastroPub, Cafe
Average price: €8-20
Area: Centrum
Address: Prinsengracht 653 1016 HV
Amsterdam The Netherlands
Phone: +31 20 6259680

#420
Solo Eten & Drinken
Category: Diners
Average price: €8-20
Area: Zuid, Museumkwartier
Address: Van Baerlestraat 35-37
1071 AP Amsterdam The Netherlands
Phone: +31 20 6622655

#421
District 5
Category: Italian, Pizza
Average price: €8-20
Area: Zuid, De Pijp
Address: Van der Helstplein 17
1073 AR Amsterdam The Netherlands
Phone: +31 20 7700884

#422
WestergasTerras
Category: Pub, Cafe
Average price: €8-20
Area: West
Address: Klönneplein 4-6 1014 DD
Amsterdam The Netherlands
Phone: +31 20 6848496

#423
Van Harte
Category: GastroPub
Average price: €8-20
Area: Centrum, Negen Straatjes
Address: Hartenstraat 24-BG 1016 CC
Amsterdam The Netherlands
Phone: +31 20 6258500

#424
Bouf
Category: French, European
Average price: €21-40
Area: Zuid, Museumkwartier
Address: Van Baerlestraat 51-I
1071 AP Amsterdam The Netherlands
Phone: +31 20 6736222

#425
Café de Vergulde Gaper
Category: GastroPub
Average price: €8-20
Area: Centrum
Address: Prinsenstraat 30 1015 DD
Amsterdam The Netherlands
Phone: +31 20 6248975

#426
Het Karbeel
Category: GastroPub
Average price: €8-20
Area: Centrum, De Wallen
Address: Warmoesstraat 16
1012 JD Amsterdam The Netherlands
Phone: +31 20 6274995

#427
St.
Category: Irish, GastroPub
Average price: €21-40
Area: Centrum
Address: Rembrandtplein 8-10
1017 CV Amsterdam The Netherlands
Phone: +31 20 4226886

#428
Kitchen & Bar Van Rijn
Category: Bar, Steakhouses
Average price: €8-20
Area: Centrum
Address: Rembrandtplein 17 1017 CT
Amsterdam The Netherlands
Phone: +31 20 4500555

#429
Café Zilt
Category: Dive Bar, Cafe
Average price: €8-20
Area: Centrum, De Wallen
Address: Zeedijk 49 1012 AR
Amsterdam The Netherlands
Phone: +31 20 4215416

#430
Kong Kha
Category: Thai
Average price: €8-20
Area: Zuid, Rivierenbuurt
Address: Rijnstraat 87 1079 GZ
Amsterdam The Netherlands
Phone: +31 20 6612578

#431
Senses restaurant
Category: French, Wine Bar
Average price: €8-20
Area: Centrum
Address: Vijzelstraat 45 1017 HE
Amsterdam The Netherlands
Phone: +31 20 5306266

#432
De Blauwe Hollander
Category: GastroPub
Average price: €8-20
Area: Centrum
Address: Leidsekruisstraat 28
1017 RJ Amsterdam The Netherlands
Phone: +31 20 6270521

#433
Brasserie Harkema
Category: French, Brasseries
Average price: €21-40
Area: Centrum, De Wallen
Address: Nes 67-69 1012 KD
Amsterdam The Netherlands
Phone: +31 20 4281111

#434
Coco's Outback
Category: Bar, Dance Club, Australian
Average price: €8-20
Area: Centrum
Address: Thorbeckeplein 8 1017 CS
Amsterdam The Netherlands
Phone: +31 20 6272423

#435
D' Overkant
Category: Pub, GastroPub, Cafe
Average price: €8-20
Area: Zuid, Rivierenbuurt
Address: Scheldestraat 101-105
1078 GJ Amsterdam The Netherlands
Phone: +31 20 6797366

#436
Cafe Fonteyn
Category: Bar, GastroPub
Average price: €8-20
Area: Centrum
Address: Nieuwmarkt 13-BG 1011 JR
Amsterdam The Netherlands
Phone: +31 20 4227050

#437
Ganesha Indian
Category: Indian
Average price: €8-20
Area: Centrum, De Wallen
Address: Geldersekade 5-BG
1011 EH Amsterdam The Netherlands
Phone: +31 20 3207302

#438
Côte Ouest Café
Category: French
Average price: €21-40
Area: Centrum
Address: Gravenstraat 20 1012 NM
Amsterdam The Netherlands
Phone: +31 20 3208998

#439
Rakang
Category: Thai
Average price: €8-20
Area: Centrum, Jordaan
Address: Elandsgracht 29-HS
1016 TM Amsterdam The Netherlands
Phone: +31 20 6275012

#440
Flinders Cafe
Category: Diners, Cafe, Sandwiches
Average price: €8-20
Area: West, Frederik Hendrikbuurt
Address: Frederik Hendrikplantsoen 36
1052 XS Amsterdam The Netherlands
Phone: +31 20 2231583

#441
Brasserie Klokspijs
Category: Brasseries
Average price: €8-20
Area: Zuid, De Pijp
Address: Hemonystraat 38 1074 BS
Amsterdam The Netherlands
Phone: +31 20 3642560

#442
Cafe de Zagerij
Category: GastroPub, Sandwiches
Average price: €8-20
Area: Centrum, Jordaan
Address: Westerstraat 182 1015 MR
Amsterdam The Netherlands
Phone: +31 20 4211155

#443
Roberto's Restaurant
Category: Italian
Average price: Above €41
Area: Zuid, Apollobuurt
Address: Apollolaan 138 1077 BG
Amsterdam The Netherlands
Phone: +31 20 7106025

#444
**Chinees Specialiteiten Restaurant
Oceania**
Category: Chinese
Average price: Above €41
Area: Zuid, Rivierenbuurt
Address: Scheldestraat 77 1078 GH
Amsterdam The Netherlands
Phone: +31 20 6738907

#445
De Hollandsche Manege
Category: Venues & Events,
Horseback Riding, Cafe
Average price: €8-20
Area: Oud West
Address: Vondelstraat 140-I 1054 GT
Amsterdam The Netherlands
Phone: +31 20 6180942

#446
Le Zinc...
Category: French
Average price: €8-20
Area: Centrum
Address: Prinsengracht 999 1017 KM
Amsterdam The Netherlands
Phone: +31 20 6229044

#447
Oresti's Taverna
Category: Tapas, Mediterranean
Average price: €8-20
Area: Zuid, De Pijp
Address: Daniel Stalpertstraat 93
1072 XD Amsterdam The Netherlands
Phone: +31 20 4222742

#448
Hesp
Category: Nightlife, GastroPub
Average price: €8-20
Area: Oost, Oosterparkbuurt
Address: Weesperzijde 130-131
1091 ER Amsterdam The Netherlands
Phone: +31 20 6651202

#449
Starbucks
Category: Coffee & Tea, Cafe
Average price: €8-20
Area: Centrum
Address: Leidsestraat 101 1017 NZ
Amsterdam The Netherlands
Phone: +31 20 6241592

#450
Cafe Marie
Category: GastroPub, European
Average price: €8-20
Area: Zuid, De Pijp
Address: Marie Heinekenplein 5
1072 MH Amsterdam The Netherlands
Phone: +31 20 2232096

#451
Café Thijssen
Category: Pub, Sandwiches
Average price: €8-20
Area: Centrum, Jordaan
Address: Brouwersgracht 107-II
1015 GD Amsterdam The Netherlands
Phone: +31 20 6238994

#452
Het Paardje
Category: GastroPub
Average price: €8-20
Area: Zuid, De Pijp
Address: Gerard Douplein 1 1073 XE
Amsterdam The Netherlands
Phone: +31 20 6643539

#453
Uliveto traiteur
Category: Italian, Do-It-Yourself Food
Average price: €21-40
Area: Centrum
Address: Weteringschans 118 1017 XT
Amsterdam The Netherlands
Phone: +31 20 4230099

#454
Boom
Category: European, French
Average price: €8-20
Area: Oost, Dapperbuurt
Address: Linnaeusstraat 63 1093 EJ
Amsterdam The Netherlands
Phone: +31 20 6655224

#455
MC Theater
Category: Caribbean
Average price: €8-20
Area: West
Address: Polonceaukade 5 1014 DA
Amsterdam The Netherlands
Phone: +31 20 4750425

#456
BIHP
Category: Art Gallery, French
Average price: €21-40
Area: Centrum, Negen Straatjes
Address: Keizersgracht 335 1016 EG
Amsterdam The Netherlands
Phone: +31 20 4282609

#457
Mercat
Category: Spanish
Average price: €21-40
Area: Oost
Address: Oostelijke Handelskade 4
1019 BM Amsterdam The Netherlands
Phone: +31 20 3446424

#458
L'Express
Category: French
Average price: €21-40
Area: Centrum
Address: Utrechtsestraat 29-4
1017 VH Amsterdam The Netherlands
Phone: +31 20 6205129

#459
Café 't Hooischip
Category: Dive Bar, GastroPub
Average price: €8-20
Area: Centrum
Address: Amstel 31 1011 PT
Amsterdam The Netherlands
Phone: +31 20 6238733

#460
Tapas Café Duende
Category: Spanish, Tapas
Average price: €8-20
Area: Centrum, Jordaan
Address: Lindengracht 62-BG
1015 KJ Amsterdam The Netherlands
Phone: +31 20 4206692

#461
Casa Del Gusto
Category: Italian, Do-It-Yourself Food,
Ethnic Food
Average price: Under €7
Area: Centrum
Address: Kerkstraat 121 1017 GE
Amsterdam The Netherlands
Phone: +31 20 3308330

#462
Restaurant Freud
Category: Mediterranean
Average price: €8-20
Area: West
Address: Spaarndammerstraat 424
1013 SZ Amsterdam The Netherlands
Phone: +31 20 6885548

#463
Saskia's Huiskamer
Category: Portuguese
Average price: €8-20
Area: Zuid, De Pijp
Address: Albert Cuypstraat 203 C
1073 BE Amsterdam The Netherlands
Phone: +31 628 629839

#464
Café Saloon
Category: Cafe
Average price: €8-20
Area: Centrum
Address: Lijnbaansgracht 271
1017 RL Amsterdam The Netherlands
Phone: +31 20 6230466

#465
Quattro Gatti
Category: Italian
Average price: €21-40
Area: Centrum, Negen Straatjes
Address: Hartenstraat 3-1 1016 BZ
Amsterdam The Netherlands
Phone: +31 20 4214585

#466
Tjin's Exotische Broodjes
Category: Bakeries, Sandwiches
Average price: Under €7
Area: Zuid, De Pijp
Address: Van Woustraat 17 1074 AA
Amsterdam The Netherlands
Phone: +31 20 6793758

#467
Hakata Senpachi
Category: Japanese
Average price: €21-40
Area: Zuid, Rivierenbuurt
Address: Wielingenstraat 16-HS
1078 KK Amsterdam The Netherlands
Phone: +31 20 6625823

#468
Himalaya New Age Shop
Category: Books, Mags,
Music & Video, Breakfast & Brunch
Average price: €8-20
Area: Centrum, De Wallen
Address: Warmoesstraat 56 1012 JG
Amsterdam The Netherlands
Phone: +31 20 6260899

#469
Eau de Vie
Category: Mediterranean, French
Average price: €21-40
Area: Zuid, Rivierenbuurt
Address: Maasstraat 20 1078 HK
Amsterdam The Netherlands
Phone: +31 20 6629588

#470
Di Sale
Category: Italian
Average price: €21-40
Area: Zuid, Museumkwartier
Address: Willemsparkweg 155 1071 GX
Amsterdam The Netherlands
Phone: +31 20 6623853

#471
Midtown Grill
Category: Steakhouses
Average price: €21-40
Area: West
Address: Stadhouderskade 12 1054 ES
Amsterdam The Netherlands
Phone: +31 20 6075529

#472
Beulings
Category: Restaurant
Average price: €21-40
Area: Centrum
Address: Beulingstraat 9-HS 1017 BA
Amsterdam The Netherlands
Phone: +31 20 3206100

#473
Restaurant Orontes
Category: Turkish
Average price: €8-20
Area: Zuid, De Pijp
Address: Albert Cuypstraat 40-BG
1072 CV Amsterdam The Netherlands
Phone: +31 20 6796225

#474
Roem
Category: Do-It-Yourself Food, GastroPub
Average price: €8-20
Area: Centrum, Jordaan
Address: Prinsengracht 126 1015 EA
Amsterdam The Netherlands
Phone: +31 20 4277955

#475
Asian Kitchen
Category: Chinese
Average price: €8-20
Area: Centrum
Address: Vijzelstraat 5 a 1017 HD
Amsterdam The Netherlands
Phone: +31 20 6201916

#476
De Blaffende Vis
Category: GastroPub
Average price: €8-20
Area: Centrum, Jordaan
Address: Westerstraat 118 1015 MN
Amsterdam The Netherlands
Phone: +31 20 6251721

#477
Proust
Category: GastroPub
Average price: €8-20
Area: Centrum, Jordaan
Address: Noordermarkt 4 1015 MV
Amsterdam The Netherlands
Phone: +31 20 6239145

#478
Eetcafé de Staalmeesters
Category: GastroPub
Average price: €8-20
Area: Centrum
Address: Kloveniersburgwal 127-HS
1011 KD Amsterdam The Netherlands
Phone: +31 20 6234218

#479
Mappa
Category: Italian
Average price: €21-40
Area: Centrum, De Wallen
Address: Nes 59 1012 KD
Amsterdam The Netherlands
Phone: +31 20 5289170

#480
L'invité le Restaurant
Category: French, Vegetarian,
Do-It-Yourself Food
Average price: Above €41
Area: Centrum, Jordaan
Address: Bloemgracht 47 1016 KD
Amsterdam The Netherlands
Phone: +31 20 5702010

#481
Orloff
Category: GastroPub
Average price: €8-20
Area: Centrum
Address: Kadijksplein 10-12 1018 AC
Amsterdam The Netherlands
Phone: +31 20 3203347

#482
Het Paleis
Category: GastroPub
Average price: €8-20
Area: Centrum
Address: Paleisstraat 16 1012 RB
Amsterdam The Netherlands
Phone: +31 20 6260600

#483
Fifteen
Category: Italian
Average price: €8-20
Area: Oost
Address: Jollemanhof 9 1019 GW
Amsterdam The Netherlands
Phone: +31 20 5095015

#484
Café Goos
Category: GastroPub
Average price: €8-20
Area: Zuid, Rivierenbuurt
Address: Maasstraat 74-BG 1078 HL
Amsterdam The Netherlands
Phone: +31 20 6793443

#485
Braque
Category: Cafe, French
Average price: €21-40
Area: Zuid, De Pijp
Address: Albert Cuypstraat 29-31
1072 CK Amsterdam The Netherlands
Phone: +31 20 6707357

#486
Stout
Category: Cafe
Average price: €8-20
Area: Centrum, Haarlemmerbuurt
Address: Haarlemmerstraat 73
1013 EL Amsterdam The Netherlands
Phone: +31 20 6163664

#487
Gent aan de Schinkel
Category: GastroPub
Average price: €8-20
Area: Zuid, Hoofddorppleinbuurt
Address: Theophile de Bockstraat 1
1058 TV Amsterdam The Netherlands
Phone: +31 20 3882851

#488
VandeMarkt
Category: French, Mediterranean
Average price: €21-40
Area: Oost
Address: Weesperzijde 144-147
1091 EZ Amsterdam The Netherlands
Phone: +31 20 4686958

#489
Het Badhuis
Category: French
Average price: €8-20
Area: Oost, Indische Buurt
Address: Javaplein 21 1095 CJ
Amsterdam The Netherlands
Phone: +31 20 6651226

#490
La Place Openbare Bibliotheek
Category: Restaurant
Average price: €8-20
Area: Centrum
Address: Oosterdokskade 143
1011 AD Amsterdam The Netherlands
Phone: +31 20 5230870

#491
Miss Korea
Category: Korean, Japanese
Average price: €8-20
Area: Zuid, De Pijp
Address: Albert Cuypstraat 66-70
1072 CW Amsterdam The Netherlands
Phone: +31 20 6790606

#492
Thrill Grill
Category: American, Burgers
Average price: €8-20
Area: Centrum, De Wallen
Address: Wolvenstraat 22 1016 EP
Amsterdam The Netherlands
Phone: +31 20 3033968

#493
Café de Groene Vlinder
Category: GastroPub
Average price: €8-20
Area: Zuid, De Pijp
Address: Albert Cuypstraat 130 1072 EA
Amsterdam The Netherlands
Phone: +31 20 4702500

#494
Eetcafé de Hut
Category: GastroPub
Average price: €8-20
Area: Zuid, Stadionbuurt
Address: Olympiaplein 132 1076 AK
Amsterdam The Netherlands
Phone: +31 20 6718426

#495
De Ponteneur
Category: GastroPub
Average price: €8-20
Area: Oost, Dapperbuurt
Address: Eerste van Swindenstraat 581
1093 LC Amsterdam The Netherlands
Phone: +31 20 6680680

#496
The Tara
Category: Bar, Irish, GastroPub
Average price: €8-20
Area: Centrum, De Wallen
Address: Rokin 89 1012 KL
Amsterdam The Netherlands
Phone: +31 20 4274657

#497
Café Van Zuylen
Category: GastroPub, European
Average price: €8-20
Area: Centrum
Address: Torensteeg 8-BG 1012 TH
Amsterdam The Netherlands
Phone: +31 20 6391055

#498
Starbikes Rental
Category: Breakfast & Brunch
Average price: Under €7
Area: Centrum
Address: De Ruyterkade 127 1011 AC
Amsterdam The Netherlands
Phone: +31 20 6203215

#499
Bombay Inn
Category: Pakistani, Indian
Average price: Under €7
Area: Centrum
Address: Lange Leidsedwarsstraat 46
1017 NL Amsterdam The Netherlands
Phone: +31 20 6241784

#500
Billy Thai
Category: Thai
Average price: Under €7
Area: Centrum, Jordaan
Address: Prinsengracht 358,
1016 JA Amsterdam The Netherlands
Phone: +31 20 3304220